# NORFOLK MARITIME HEROES AND LEGENDS

*Further details of Poppyland Publishing titles can be found at*
**www.poppyland.co.uk**
*where clicking on the 'Support and Resources' button
will lead to pages specially compiled to support this book*

MARK NICHOLLS

# Norfolk Maritime Heroes & Legends

POPPYLAND
PUBLISHING

ISBN 978 0 946148 85 1

Published by Poppyland Publishing, Cromer NR27 9AN

The author would like to thank the following for their help, advice, support and encouragement: Rosemary Dixon, The 3rd Lord Fisher, Patrick Fisher, Doreen Hague, Simon Harris, Andrew Lambert, John Lawson, Dominick Harrod, Trevor Heaton, Sharon Nicholls, Christopher Pipe, Steve Snelling, Peter Stibbons, David Taylor, John Taylor, Jim Watts, Pauline Weinstein and Colin White.

*Picture credits:*
*Eastern Daily Press:* pages 8 (left), 24, 47, 54 (top), 61, 98, 105, 110, 113, 122, 127, 138
R. Fiske: pages 14, 35, 57, 69, 71, 75, 76, 86, 92, 94, 95, 96
J. Inglesby: page 100
Lowestoft and East Suffolk Maritime Society: page 142
National Maritime Museum: pages 17, 22, 23, 32, 56
Norwich Castle Museum and Art Gallery: page 80 and front cover
P&O: es 163, 164, 165
Poppyland collection: pages 26, 62, 65, 83, 107, 118, 119, 131, 144, 146
Poppyland Photos: pages 8 (right), 15, 20, 28, 36, 41, 44, 45, 48, 53, 54 (bottom), 58, 66, 72, 74, 77, 87, 102, 114, 125, 128, 141, 148
Port of Lowestoft Research Society: pages 132, 133, 135, 139
Randall/Salter magic lantern slide collection: pages 84, 90
Royal National Lifeboat Institution: pages 150, 151, 152, 153, 154
Royal National Mission to Deep Sea Fishermen: page 136
J. Taylor: pages 156, 159, 160

Designed and typeset in 11½ on 14 pt Adobe Caslon
by Watermark, Cromer NR27 9HL

Printed by Barnwell's, Aylsham

*In memory of my father*
*Leslie John Nicholls*
*(1933–2007)*

# Contents

# Introduction

Norfolk has a long and illustrious maritime tradition, producing naval heroes and legends across the centuries. The county also has a proud record of maritime innovation and of providing ships and crews to serve the nation in its hour of need. As early as 1340, Yarmouth became renowned when for the Battle of Sluys it provided more ships for King Edward III's fleet to fight against the Dutch than London did, with the Yarmouth mariner John Perbroune taking command at the battle.

The county has also been recorded in the names of Royal Navy vessels across the years. There have been six HMS *Norfolk*s, though the name is not currently in use by the navy – the last vessel to bear the name, a Type 23 frigate, was sold to the Chilean navy in November 2006 and renamed the *Almirante Cochrane*. HMS *Yarmouth*, decommissioned in 1986, also played a critical role in the Falklands War of 1982. The Type 12 frigate, however, came to a sad and ill-befitting end: towed out into the North Atlantic in 1987, she was used as target practice by HMS *Manchester*, which eventually sank her.

In the maritime history of Norfolk, one name dominates that of all others: Vice Admiral Horatio Nelson. Born at Burnham Thorpe on 29th September 1758, he was undoubtedly Norfolk's greatest maritime hero through his achievements at the Battle of Trafalgar of 21st October 1805 and his earlier successes at the Nile, Cape St Vincent and numerous other heroic skirmishes. Indeed he is Britain's greatest naval hero.

Yet his connections with Norfolk, a county he loved and referred to at every opportunity with pride and affection, have in some ways eclipsed the gallant feats and innovation of many others from Norfolk who have made memorable and lasting contributions to Britain's colourful maritime history. Some have been Nelson's followers, benefiting from his patronage; others had already placed Norfolk on the maritime map of Britain long before the Vice Admiral's birth. They included seagoing warriors such as Sir Christopher Myngs or the high-ranking but ill-fated Admiral Sir Cloudesley Shovell. There are those who explored the globe, plotted new routes and charted seaways where no others had been before, such as King's Lynn-born Captain George Vancouver and, later, Samuel Gurney Cresswell.

There are those who rarely or never went to sea, yet left a lasting nautical imprint because of their contribution to the spiritual life of sailors or whose innovations and inventions helped make the sea a safer place for those who lived, worked and fought offshore.

The rather eccentric Captain George Manby, an under-recognised army officer whose weird and wonderful inventions paved the way for the establishment of maritime rescue, is one of note. Later, once the Royal National Lifeboat Institution was established, men of Norfolk were among the bravest ever to man the rescue vessels – heroes such as Henry Blogg or William Fleming. Both of these received the George Cross and the Lifeboatman's VC, the Gold Medal. There are other Norfolk mariners who were honoured with the Victoria Cross for their selfless bravery in combat, some of it in the most unexpected locations.

Norfolk also has links with mariners who shaped the Royal Navy of the 20th century, men whose drive brought in the fearful *Dreadnought* fleet of ships or left an impact on the significant military events of the century. Others contributed to a more leisurely pace of life afloat, such as the father of the boating holiday on the Norfolk Broads or the Commodore of a magnificent fleet of cruise liners.

In addition, there are many others who served at sea, often in the most appalling and treacherous conditions, who remain anonymous. While not named or recorded in this book, they are saluted through its content. These maritime heroes and legends are all men of Norfolk and, as Lord Nelson would have stated, gloried in being so. This book endeavours to recognise their feats and achievements and bring them out of the immense shadow of Lord Nelson.

CHAPTER ONE

# Sir Christopher Myngs

## (1625–1666)

Sir Christopher Myngs was a charismatic, swashbuckling hero, a seagoing warrior of the old school of mariners. He came from a generation of captains who sailed the fine line between privateering and common piracy in the days of the mid-17th century when the great seafaring nations were carving up the globe for commercial gain. Against this backdrop, seamen such as Myngs were permitted to amass significant personal fortunes from their perilous seaborne exploits whilst simultaneously serving the interests of their country and their monarch. There was often a conflict of interest, yet when it suited, this was overlooked in an age where rulers and allegiances changed with the wind.

Myngs learned his trade as a young seaman in this era. But his potential – and his usefulness to the English crown – was soon realised as he rose through the ranks. His lucrative and destabilising attacks on Spanish strongholds to raid their treasures, often unofficial and unsanctioned, carried with them a significant political benefit for England.

Among the great maritime heroes that Norfolk produced over the centuries, Sir Christopher Myngs may not be remembered in the way his counterpart Horatio Nelson is or recorded with the same reverence in the history of naval warfare. Yet there is an eerie, almost bizarre, link between them in their hour of death. Despite their differing styles, and the two sailors being separated by perhaps four generations, that coincidence is as surprising as it is tragic. Lord Nelson was not the first great Norfolk admiral to die after being shot by an enemy sniper from the rigging whilst on the deck of an English flagship named

13

the *Victory*. Almost 140 years before Nelson fell mortally wounded at the Battle of Trafalgar, Sir Christopher Myngs suffered a similar fate while in command of the warship of the age that carried the proud name of *Victory*. His opponents on that day were not the Spanish or the French, but the Dutch.

Born at Salthouse in north Norfolk, Myngs had worked his way through the ranks of the Royal Navy to Admiral by the time his flagship was brought into play during the latter part of an epic four-day battle with the Dutch fleet during the Second Dutch War of 1664–67. The Four Days Battle, as it became known, raged from 1st to 4th June 1666. Conducted off the English and Flemish coastline, it was one of the longest sea battles in early maritime history but was eventually to go the way of the Dutch. By the time it was over, the English had been heavily defeated, suffering the loss of 17 ships and 8,000 men with Sir Christopher Myngs among the mortally wounded. He was one of two admirals and ten captains to die.

On the fourth day of the battle, Myngs was broadside with the *Ridderschap* under the command of the Dutch admiral Jan De Liefde. Under intense attack, Myngs sought to ram the enemy vessel with a fire ship but this was unsuccessful and, soon after, two more Dutch warships engaged the *Victory*. As the ships closed, Myngs was shot in the throat by a Dutch marksman high in the rigging of the enemy vessel. Wounded, he stayed in

*Boys in Salthouse in Sir Christopher's day observed the ships, perhaps owned or crewed by their fathers. When they should have been concentrating on lessons in church they carved these graffiti in the choir stalls. The accurate detail in their pictures shows that they were as interested in shipping as modern boys might be in cars, and probably dreamed of having a ship of their own. Their pictures show sails furled (as they would have been seen in harbour), and many flags, as perhaps youngsters always like to put in their pictures. The high fore and stern castles are typical of Myngs' period and before.*

*Salthouse church, the place of Myngs' baptism, stands on ground well above today's village, with the sea in the background. The three admirals Myngs, Narborough and Shovell all came from this part of north Norfolk.*

command but was shot again in the neck and had to be taken below. That left a young lieutenant, John Narborough – another Norfolk man – to take command. He skilfully steered the *Victory* to relative safety but Myngs was already mortally wounded.

Myngs, or as his name was occasionally spelt Mings, was born in the manor house at Salthouse and baptised in the village in 1625, the year King Charles I ascended the throne. He grew up against the backdrop of the English Civil War and the Commonwealth under Oliver Cromwell, developing his naval career during that period before the restoration of the monarchy with Charles II in 1660. Inevitably, the England that Myngs served was quite different from that of Norfolk's greatest naval hero, Horatio Nelson, almost a century and a half later. But Myngs was at the vanguard of a great Norfolk naval tradition. He was the first of an illustrious triumvirate of 17th-century north Norfolk admirals who were to play a key part in the English navy of the time. One of his protégés was Narborough, the other was Sir Cloudesley Shovell.

Myngs joined the navy as a cabin boy, possibly in the mid-1640s, but he first came to prominence as the captain of the *Elisabeth* in action against the Dutch in the First Anglo-Dutch War. The Dutch Wars – 1652–54, 1664–67 and 1672–74 – were a series of conflicts with their roots in Anglo-Dutch commercial rivalry, although the last of the three wars was more widely based with French interests playing a primary role.

From 1655 Myngs took command of the *Marston Moor*, a vessel whose crew were supposed to be on the verge of mutiny. With firm command, Myngs brought his wayward crew into line and in 1656 arrived in Jamaica as captain of the 44-gun frigate. From there, he took part in raids in what are now Colombia and Venezuela. Over the three years that followed, with uncertainty back home in England, he raided the Spanish strongholds along the coast of South America, developing a reputation for extreme and even unnecessary cruelty as he sacked town after town. While Myngs was operating as a 'commerce raider', the Spanish considered him nothing short of a mass murderer and a pirate and consequently protested to Oliver Cromwell's government over the nature and frequency of his raids.

As the scourge of the Spanish, he mercilessly continued to plunder their treasures and by 1659 his haul was estimated at £300,000. But Myngs refused to give the government a share and instead he split the proceeds with the buccaneers under his command. Described by the English commander in Jamaica Edward D'Oyley, as 'unhinged and out of tune', he was arrested and sent back to England to be tried for the offence. Fortunately for Myngs, the political situation at home was changing rapidly. Amid the confusion and uncertainty as the Commonwealth disintegrated, Charles II became king, the charges against Myngs were dropped and he was allowed to return to Jamaica with his fleet of ships and buccaneers to continue his work against the Spanish.

Myngs was popular and gaining national renown for his feats, to the extent that the great diarist Samuel Pepys was to refer to him in his writings. Pepys also felt Myngs a figure important enough to require his presence at his funeral a few years later.

Towards the end of 1662 and aboard the *Centurion*, Myngs captured Santiago, blowing up its fortress and taking six ships. In February 1663 his forces captured San Francisco in the Bay of Campeche, seizing 14 Spanish ships and their treasure. Among his comrades were such notable captains as Edward Mansfield, Abraham Blauvelt, John Morris, Jack Rackam and Henry Morgan (1635–1688), one of the most infamous English privateers ever placed in command of a ship. It was from Myngs that Morgan truly learned his trade in these attacks of 1663. However, for Myngs, these lucrative plunderings in the Caribbean came to an end in April 1663 after the Spanish protested so strongly to the English government that Charles II forbade any further assaults. He had also sustained a wound in the attack on Campeche Bay and that meant a return to England to recover.

Until that time, the English authorities seemed content with the activities of the buccaneers and even encouraged them. The authorities in London were well aware that the country's prosperity rested on an ability to expand trading markets at a time that Spain had claimed the New World as its own. It was the activities of these privateers in undermining the Spanish grip on this part of the world that at the time were best serving the national interest of the King of England. There

*Sir Christopher Myngs in a grand portrait by Sir Peter Lely. It is one of the set known as 'The Flagmen of Lowestoft', twelve paintings of admirals and captains who fought in the second Anglo-Dutch war.*

remained a very fine line between privateering and outright piracy but attitudes towards Spain were still tinged by the threat it had posed to English national security 70 years earlier as the Spanish Armada sailed on England and was only repelled through the exploits of Sir Francis Drake.

The England of 1665, when Myngs was recovering from his wounds, was a nation facing difficult times. The Dutch Wars were again occupying naval forces at sea while on land the Great Plague was ravaging the country. England had emerged the stronger from the first wars but the Dutch continued to challenge English commercial supremacy. In response, Dutch colonies were raided on the coast of Africa and America, inevitably leading to a second declaration of war.

It was during the second of these conflicts (1664–67) that Sir Christopher Myngs served his country best. His fine vessel, the *Victory*, had been taken to pieces and rebuilt at Chatham as a 2nd Rate ship of 1,029 tons and carrying a crew of 500. She was not the same ship that Nelson sailed at Trafalgar (his HMS *Victory* was launched in 1765). But during the Second Dutch War the rebuilt 82-gunner became a highly effective flagship commanded by the recently promoted Vice Admiral Christopher Myngs.

In June 1665 the Duke of York – later King James II – won the Battle of Lowestoft, with Myngs and the *Victory* playing an important role. The battle ended in a decisive victory for the English and Myngs was knighted for his services and then ordered with a squadron of ships to guard the critical Channel trade routes. Despite that success, the English fleet failed to take advantage and press home its dominance. In January 1666 another factor came into play as Louis XIV of France declared war on England, though at that stage took little effective part in the Anglo-Dutch conflict.

By June 1666, English and Dutch forces were again locked in battle at sea in a skirmish that was to lead to a major naval setback. Under the supreme fleet commander George Monck and Prince Rupert, the English were badly defeated in the Four Days Battle. It was Myngs' last battle: the bullet wounds he sustained on the deck of his flagship led to his death a week later, at the age of 41.

Admiral Sir Christopher Myngs led a life that was daring, dramatic, violent and lucrative. He amassed a fortune from Spanish raids but also gained a reputation as an effective leader in the thick of naval battle. It was a life spent in near constant conflict at sea.

In north Norfolk, his name is remembered in the village of Salthouse as that of a great sailor from the county. For a few years, his name was recalled following the Great Floods of 1953, which devastated homes and communities along the north Norfolk coastline and left 100 people dead. Temporary homes to house flood-hit families were constructed in a row named Myngs Terrace, but these were knocked down in the late 1990s.

Myngs was one of the first great Norfolk admirals, a man who acquired substantial wealth as a privateer and a sailor who died serving his country.

CHAPTER TWO

# Sir John Narborough

## (1640–1688)

Sir John Narborough ocupies a curious place in Norfolk's naval history. He is the critical link between two other famous north Norfolk seamen: Sir Christopher Myngs, a privateer and patriot of the first order; and the establishment figure of Sir Cloudesley Shovell, who rose to become the second highest ranking sailor in the land. But Narborough is worthy of note in his own right, for his service in the Dutch Wars and an expedition to the South Seas where his survey pinpointed key points on the Patagonian coast. Eventually rising to the rank of Rear Admiral, he was a highly able seaman, a competent navigator and popular with his crews for his steadfast insistence that his ships be 'maintained and furnished' in the best of order with good provisions readily available for his men.

Descended from an old Norfolk family (the name is sometimes spelled Narbrough), he is the lynchpin that holds the trio of 17th-century Norfolk admirals together, the three being of particular interest because of their common origins from a small area of the north Norfolk coastline. Narborough and his protégé Shovell originate from Cockthorpe, while Myngs, who undoubtedly assisted Narborough in his early career, came from close by at Salthouse. Little is known about Narborough's early life, but his roots can be traced back to Cockthorpe, where he was christened on 11th October 1640, and regularly worshiped at All Saints' church in the village.

He received his commission in 1664 and in 1666 was promoted lieutenant for gallantry in the action with the Dutch fleet at the Four Days' Battle under the service of Myngs aboard his flagship.

*Cockthorpe church, now in the care of the Norfolk Churches Trust, has links with both Narborough and Shovell.*

It was at the height of the longest battle of the second of the Dutch Wars (1664–1667) that Lieutenant Narborough achieved recognition. With Myngs mortally wounded, it fell to Narborough to negotiate a path to safety for the 82-gun *Victory* under heavy enemy fire.

By the time it was over, the English, under Prince Rupert, were badly defeated, suffering the loss of 17 ships and 8,000 men but Narborough survived to lead another day.

After peace was negotiated, Narborough was chosen to conduct a voyage of exploration in the South Seas, sailing from Deptford on 26th November 1669. After exploring the coast of Patagonia, he entered the Strait of Magellan and the Pacific Ocean in November 1670. The voyage took him along the coast of Chile as far as Valdivia where he was confronted by Spanish authorities who refused him entry to the harbour, effectively bringing an end to the expedition.

A narrative of the expedition was published at London in 1694 under the grandiose title *An Account of Several Late Voyages and Discoveries to the South and North*. It was able to show that Narborough recorded the exact geographical position of the principal points on the Patagonian coasts and the Strait of Magellan. The work was widely respected by sailors passing through that part of the world and was extensively used for nearly a century afterwards.

Narborough was a man who had much to offer the navy: his navigational skills were significantly more advanced than those of many of his contemporaries, and he was popular with his crews. Records show that in 1672, for example, he was 'warmly cheered' by crews of the fleet.

During the Third Anglo-Dutch War, Narborough was second captain of the Lord High Admiral's ship. His valour was recognised at the Battle of Solebay (Southwold Bay) in May 1672; and in autumn 1673, for his service in the campaign, he was made rear admiral and knighted. The following year he was despatched to the Mediterranean as commander-in-chief.

Narborough demonstrated a concern for his crew's well-being and was keen to secure the best provisions. He would meticulously note what came aboard. Lying at Nore in 1672, for example, he wrote in his log:

> This day fresh meat came down for the whole fleet and a vessel laden with 3950 cabbages and 21 and a half bushels of carrots and 15 dozen and 9 bunches of turnips, for to be disposed for the use of the fleet in the several ships for refreshing of the men.

> I made a dividend of my carrots and cabbages and turnips to the whole fleet, a cabbage for four men and a bushel of carrots for ten men.

There was a sense of fairness in the way Narborough supplied his crews, officers never having first choice or better cuts than the men of the crew. In another passage he notes:

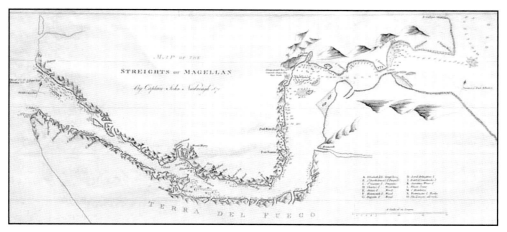

*'Map of the Streights of Magellan by Capt. John Narbrough 1670', published by James Burney in 1807 in his* History of the Voyages and Discoveries in the South Sea or Pacific Ocean.

© National Maritime Museum, Greenwich, London

*Narborough led the attack on Tripoli, which was intended to curb the piracy of the Algerian pirates. The younger Cloudesley Shovell was a lieutenant aboard the* Henrietta.

> Today the cooper found two butts of beer had leaked out: this day all of us drank water only, for it was ever my order that the meanest boy in the ship should have the same allowance with my self, so that in general we all drank of the same cask, and ate one sort of provisions, as long as they lasted. I never permitted any officer to have a better piece of meat than what fell to his lot.

Narborough also insisted his men wash daily and remain free from lice to ensure they remained healthy, active and reliable members of the crew.

He commanded the expeditions against Tripoli in 1675, where he was sent to suppress acts of piracy with his compatriot from Norfolk, Cloudesley Shovell. The younger man had become a second lieutenant aboard Narborough's flagship the *Henrietta* in 1673. Indeed, it was Shovell who led the successful attack on Tripoli in 1676 with a daring boat raid on 14th January to burn four men-of-war in the harbour. Narborough later sank four more in open seas, persuading the local ruler, the Dey, to sign a meaningful peace treaty.

Later, Narborough undertook a similar expedition against the Algerines in 1677, though was hampered by poor supplies, a fact that would have irked him greatly.

# CHAPTER THREE

# Sir Cloudesley Shovell

## (1650–1707)

'Cloudesley' is an unusual Christian name even for the second half of the 17th century. It was to set the man apart as he rose not only through the social classes but also the ranks of the Royal Navy to become one of the highest ranking sailors in the land. Yet his life, and career, ended in tragedy when a navigational error – for which he was ultimately responsible through rank and command – saw the loss of five British warships and 2,000 men. For a man who is regarded by enthusiasts as possibly the finest seaman of Queen Anne's age, this was an ignominious end to a successful career and it is perhaps because of this disaster that Cloudesley Shovell is not feted across the pages of history in the way that he perhaps should be.

At the time of his death, in his 57th year, when HMS *Association* struck Gilstone Rock near the Isles of Scilly on the night of 22nd/23rd October 1707, he was the second most senior naval officer in Britain. While the maritime disaster was a direct result of a navigational fault, it is also one that can be blamed to a reasonable degree on the limitations of the technology available at the time rather than outright human error. It was also an age where naval officers were responsible for providing their own navigational equipment, and as a consequence there was inconsistency in the quality of what was in use from one ship to another.

However, the scale of the disaster did trigger the race to solve the great navigational riddle that faced all sailors of the time – of how to measure longitude. Something better than 'dead reckoning' was needed to navigate dangerous waters, and the Longitude Act of 1714 was drawn up by Parliament to offer a large

*A depiction of the tragedy in 1707 as the fleet, returning from the Mediterranean, made a fatal error of navigation and found itself amongst the rocks off the Isles of Scilly.*

monetary prize to anyone who could devise a method for determining longitude accurately at sea. This was a puzzle finally solved by 18th-century engineer John Harrison with his H4 marine chronometer clock in the years after Shovell's death.

Sir Cloudesley Shovell was born at Cockthorpe in north Norfolk and christened on 25th November 1650, at All Saints' church in the village. The unusual Christian name is derived from his maternal grandmother, who was Lucy Cloudesley. Shovell was a man who came from a simple country background, the son of yeoman farmer John Shovell, and educated in Norfolk schools to a standard where he could read and write.

From an early age he was brought up to work with small ships and was described as a 'tarpaulin', having been trained thoroughly in the rudiments of how to sail a ship. This gave him a significant advantage over his contemporary officers. Shovell knew his way around a ship and could ably handle a vessel. There were more than a handful of senior officers in service at the time who did not possess that level of competency.

Physically, Shovell was a big man. He had a large head on his shoulders and within it, a naval brain to match. Diplomatic, charismatic and popular with his crews, he was the kind of leader who liked to be amongst the action and was admired for his bravery. Despite his humble Norfolk beginnings, Shovell was a man comfortable in dealing with senior people from other nations, even those with royal connections.

The young Shovell was also fortunate to enjoy the patronage of those two other great north Norfolk seamen, Sir Christopher Myngs and Sir John Narborough. As a boy, Cloudesley Shovell – or Clowdisley Shovell as his name was occasionally spelled – joined a ship commanded by Myngs and went on his first voyage in 1662 to the West Indies. He was probably involved in the battles of the Dutch Wars and may even have seen Myngs suffer the wound that was to lead to his death in the Four Days' Battle of June 1666.

In the autumn of 1673 he became second lieutenant aboard the *Henrietta*, the flagship of the other 'admiral from Cockthorpe', Sir John Narborough. Narborough, who died in 1688, was a man he was to serve with and respect, and he even married his widow in 1691. The Narboroughs' boys, John and James, went down with Shovell as the *Association* foundered.

In his youth Shovell carved out a reputation as a seaman, taking part in a successful attack on Tripoli in 1676 before receiving his first independent command as captain of the 32-gun *Sapphire* in 1677. By 1689, a veteran of the Second and Third Dutch Wars, he was rear admiral of the blue commanding HMS *Edgar* at the Battle of Bantry Bay. In the early 1690s he fought in the War of the Spanish Succession and the War of the Grand Alliance, defeating the French in the battle of La Hogue. He was at the Battle of Barfleur in 1692, Battle of Malaga in 1704 and the 1705 capture of Barcelona, having earlier destroyed the Spanish silver fleet off Vigo. At the time of his death in 1707 he was the Rear Admiral of Great Britain, the second highest naval officer in the country.

During this period and already one of Britain's great maritime heroes, Sir Cloudesley had the misfortune to be at sea when the Great Storm of 1703 struck on the night of 26th/27th November. It was one of the worst storms on record in Britain; church steeples crashed to the ground, chimneys toppled and thousands of people lost their lives, many on the open sea. At one time 500 British vessels were reported to be in serious trouble, with Shovell aboard one of them. Shovell, who had been elected MP for Rochester in 1695, was feared missing, though he eventually turned up safely.

Yet there were also low points to his naval career. Apart from the failure of the attack on the key French naval base of Toulon and the loss of the *Association* and other ships on the return in 1707, another great disappointment in his career was the loss of a convoy that was to be taken to Smyrna in 1693. It was captured by the French, as much by the carelessness of senior officers as by the guile of the enemy. Shovell survived with his reputation intact, fortunate not to have his career ruined as a result, with others higher up the chain of command carrying the ultimate blame and subsequent shame. Shovell, who was a devout Christian,

*A visit to the Isles of Scilly offers a variety of opportunities for boat trips amongst the small islands and rocks east of Bishop Rock. In a time when the measurement of longitude was far from precise because of the lack of exact timekeeping, sailing into these waters at night often led to disaster. The Gilstone Rock just peeps above the water.*

came through this debacle and managed to retain the respect of his superiors as well as his subordinates.

In the style of Nelson a century later, he was a good man manager and motivational leader, recognising the benefits of treating his crews well. He rarely had difficulty in manning his ships as a result. His success as a captain and commander also meant that there was always the possibility of prize money for those who sailed and served alongside him.

It was on the return journey from the abortive attack on Toulon on that bleak night in late October 1707 that Sir Cloudesley Shovell met his demise, wrecked off the Isles of Scilly with the loss of the core of his fleet and up to 2,000 men. Amid the fog, the ships under Sir Cloudesley are feared to have misjudged their position, coming to grief on the treacherous rocks of the Isles of Scilly. There is a story which suggests a crewman spotted the navigational error and made his fears known to senior officers but the advice was ignored and the sailor hanged for his insubordination. However, Shovell authorities doubt the truth of this, pointing to a lack of evidence and also to the fact that it would have been quite out of character for Shovell to punish a crew member in such a brutal and off-hand manner in such circumstances.

On that night of 22nd October 1707, the 21 ships of Shovell's fleet thought they were in the eastern approach of the English Channel, in an area of sea near Cornwall and Scilly and off the French coast area of Ushant. Having been away for 18 months and thinking they were in the mouth of the Channel, there was an enthusiasm and urgency to get home. Tragically, the ships were not where they thought they were.

The reason lies in the imprecision of early 18th-century navigation. Latitude was measured by a backstaff and though the weather was bad it is believed some ships did get a sight reading. The determination of longitude was inexact, hence the quest by Harrison to find a solution. Compasses were poor and charts were inaccurate. Shovell was also persuaded by those closest to him that they were on a valid course and could sail on into the night and home. But it was a grave error. Ships lost included the *Association*, *Eagle*, *Romney* and *Firebrand*; the *Phoenix* had to be beached.

Shovell's demise is also surrounded by another mystery – that of his missing emerald ring. There are also differing accounts of how he met his death. One version suggests the flagship, HMS *Association*, foundered first and sank within minutes with all aboard seemingly drowned. Shovell was swept overboard; his body was discovered eight miles away in Porthellick Cove on St Mary's Island by a passing woman. Noting his emerald ring, instead of reviving the admiral, she murdered him for it, only confessing her crime to a minister on her deathbed three decades later. This tale emerged towards the end of the 18th century as a family story through the Marshams (via Elizabeth Shovell) and a grandson of Shovell.

The family's version of events differed slightly, suggesting that Shovell with Edmund Loades, John and James Narborough and the ship's whippet initially escaped from the sinking *Association*, perhaps in the Admiral's barge. It seems the barge broke up and the bodies were washed ashore. Shovell was discovered on the beach, his rings removed and his body buried in the sand before it was dug up a few days later, with the rings missing.

The rings later appear in the ownership of the Berkeley family, allegedly given to James, earl of Berkeley by the confessional minister. Berkeley was the same James Dursley who had been captain of the *St George*, a vessel that had escaped with minimal damage on the night of 22nd October 1707. The emerald ring was traced as recently as 1942 but by that time it had been shaped into a locket. It is believed the remnants of the ring may still exist, possibly in the United States.

The events surrounding Sir Cloudesley's death cast a shadow over what was a distinguished career, 'a proper naval career' – learning his trade, rising through the ranks and retaining the trust and respect of his men. Yet ultimately the greatest sailor of Queen Anne's age died as a result of a professional mistake. For his rank and his achievements, Shovell has been treated unfairly in the annals of British maritime history and admirers believe his feats have not been recognised in the way they should have been.

He was, however, afforded a magnificent tomb in Westminster Abbey though few revere it in the way they do the final resting places of other maritime greats. Indeed, the 300th anniversary of Shovell's demise on 22nd October 2007 was not marked with widespread commemorations. There was a simple wreath-laying at his tomb organised by the 1805 Club and the Britannia Naval Research Association, some commemorative events and lectures on the Isles of Scilly and a small dinner in his honour in a local pub close to where he was born, but little else. What those locals from Norfolk, who have formed the Shovell Dinner Committee, also did in memory of the mariner was to raise a toast to the Admiral with a glass filled with a 'Sir Cloudesley' – a concoction, created in the 18th century, of beer laced with brandy and seasoned with lemon juice and cane sugar. The small group from north Norfolk was also among those placing a wreath on Sir Cloudesley's tomb in Westminster Abbey. The note on it was simple. It read: 'to our Admiral'.

of the *Norwich Mercury*. The boy would also undoubtedly have been aware of the pledge Maurice Suckling had made to his father a few years earlier during the difficult period the family had endured over Christmas 1767. It was a woeful time for the Nelson and Suckling families; on 26th December Nelson's mother Catherine – Maurice Suckling's sister – died. Horatio was nine at the time, the sixth child of the 11 children Catherine bore Edmund. Within a fortnight, on 6th January 1768, Nelson's grandmother Anna Suckling – Maurice's own mother – was dead. Maurice, who lived at Woodton Hall nine miles south of Norwich, had hurried to Burnham Thorpe to help with the funeral arrangements and support the family as best he could.

Captain Suckling would have been familiar with the village parsonage where Horatio was born on 29th September 1758, and All Saints' church where Edmund Nelson was rector. He would perhaps still recognise it today. In many ways, Burnham Thorpe has changed little since the time of Nelson. The church stands timelessly on the hill and the River Burn – now closer to a flowing stream – still runs nearby. The pub, known as The Plough when Lord Nelson held a farewell party in 1793 after five years ashore, is as the Vice Admiral and Suckling would recognise, apart from it now bearing Nelson's name.

The parsonage, which stood some way from the church, was knocked down in 1803. Only a plaque on the wall in Creake Road bears testimony that this was where Nelson, Britain's 'greatest naval hero', was born. But the churchyard hosts the tomb of Nelson's sister Susannah Bolton, while the tombs of his parents Edmund and Catherine are below a bust of the Vice Admiral near the altar inside All Saints' church.

During that stay, Captain Suckling had time to talk to the rector about how his family would cope and what he could do to help. In conversation, he told Edmund Nelson that he would take one of his elder boys to sea at the earliest opportunity and do all he could to support the young man's career.

The youngster turned out to be the enthusiastic, albeit somewhat slight, Horatio. But Nelson was fortunate to have such a patron. Maurice was a naval officer of status, a man of considerable influence, well connected both socially and within military and political circles. Indeed, Maurice and Catherine Suckling (1725–67) were the grand nephew and grand niece of the politician Sir Robert Walpole (1676–1745), the first British Prime Minister and the man who had Houghton Hall built. They were similarly related to Sir Robert's younger brother, the naval captain Galfridus Walpole (1684–1726) who had gained renown for his exploits at Vido Bay in the Mediterranean in March 1711 as captain of HMS *Lion* when it had been engaged by four French warships. Captain Walpole, also Norfolk-born, lost his right arm after being hit by a cannon ball during the exchange.

Intriguingly, a sword Captain Walpole carried at the time was to become something of a family heirloom, passed down through the naval thread in the Suckling and Nelson families. In time, it came into the possession of Captain Maurice Suckling who was later to hand it on to his younger brother William (1729–98). At some point William gave it to Horatio Nelson, who is believed to have been in possession of it when he lost his own right arm in a skirmish on Tenerife in 1797. The sword returned to the Suckling family when Nelson arrived at Yarmouth in 1800, with the party that included Emma Hamilton, and presented it to William's son, Lieutenant Maurice William Suckling (1761–1820).

Some four years after the deaths of Catherine and Anna Suckling, Captain Maurice Suckling plucked the young Horatio from the rural Norfolk idyll of Burnham Thorpe for his first experience of life at sea. By the age of 12 Horatio was keen to go, though Suckling did initially have reservations and wrote to the pastor of his concerns about Horatio's suitability for the rough life aboard ship. Indeed, he wrote:

> What has poor Horace done, who is so weak, that he above all the rest should be sent to rough it at sea? But let him come and the first time we go into action a cannonball may knock off his head and provide for him at once.

Duly, Horatio did set out to Chatham in the Spring of 1771 and joined the *Raisonable*, which had earlier been captured from the French. The vessel was one of the ships being mobilised for a possible war with Spain over the Falkland Islands.

Life at sea began well down the rankings of the British Navy for Horatio Nelson. He may have had powerful and influential patrons but he started as a mere 'captain's servant'. A man who was eventually to give some of the most lucid and inspired orders ever issued at sea certainly learned how to take them in his early days aboard.

Nelson never, in fact, saw action under his uncle. When the *Raisonable* was stood down and Suckling moved to the *Triumph*, he secured a passage for the young Horatio to the West Indies on a vessel commanded by one of his petty officers. It gave Nelson a perfect insight into seafaring skills, mooring and maintaining the rigging.

In July 1772, Nelson rejoined Suckling on the *Triumph* and during his year off Medway he improved his knowledge of sailing and learned pilotage of the Thames estuary, though he took an early dislike to the brutality of life on board.

It was Suckling who secured Nelson a place on one of the warships, HMS

*Carcass*, that was to accompany a scientific expedition to the Arctic and later his position on HMS *Seahorse* to the Indian Ocean. In his early naval years, Nelson served on a number of ships in the East and West Indies, America and the North Sea, making steady promotion wherever he went, charting the course that would eventually lead to his finest hour at Trafalgar.

Suckling used his growing influence to steer Nelson's career as best he could, right up until his death, by identifying opportunities for him to improve his seamanship and gain wider experience of life at sea. He also selected the right ships for him to serve on with the best officers in the most advantageous stations.

Suckling went on to become Comptroller of the Navy (chairman of the Navy Board) in 1775, which was regarded as an important administrative position. However, he was not as effective as he might have been with his career curtailed by serious illness. He died, one week before the battle of Ushant, in July 1778.

Suckling, without doubt, was the man who had most influenced Nelson's early career by paving the way for his progression, though there were times in later life that Nelson played down that level of influence. However, while publicly preferring to foster the impression that he had made it to the top of his profession unaided, he did acknowledge the contribution Maurice had made to his career in private family letters.

*Woodton Hall in 1842.*

35

After Maurice's death, Nelson was not left without a powerful family patron. His uncle and Maurice's brother, William Suckling, was by that stage Deputy Collector of Customs. He was well connected at the War Office and also had the ear of the Prime Minister, Lord North.

It was William Suckling who managed to secure Nelson's command of the *Albermarle* in 1781. In a letter to William in July 1786, Nelson acknowledged with a degree of affection Maurice's contribution to his career. He wrote: 'I shall prove myself, by my actions, worthy of supplying that place in the Service of my country, which my dear uncle left for me.'

Captain Maurice Suckling's support and patronage of Nelson as he guided his career during his early period at sea was to prove critical all those years later in 1805 at the Battle of Trafalgar. Although Suckling's finest hour in 1757 occurred almost a year before Nelson's birth, the Vice Admiral was aware of his uncle's heroics from an early age. Indeed, it would have inspired him and would have been a source of strength and comfort, and the significance of meeting the enemy off Trafalgar on 21st October 1805, would not have been lost on Horatio Nelson.

*A visit to Burnham Thorpe churchyard reveals that the name of Suckling is still to be found in the area.*

# CHAPTER FIVE

# *James Burney*

## (1750–1821)

James Burney's early life at sea was one of adventure. It started when he was barely ten years old on journeys that would take him half way across the globe. Within a few years, a place was obtained for him on the momentous expeditions of Captain James Cook to the Antarctic. He was aboard ships at the forefront of exploration, on high profile sailings that were the most important missions of the time. Yet the potential offered from those early opportunities was never fully realised by Burney and his naval career seemed to founder when he was still in his mid-30s. Illness had hampered his opportunity for further commands in the Royal Navy, though an error of judgement on a sailing to India in the early 1780s haunted him for much of the remainder of his life, along with an unfashionable Republican stance that did little to endear him to those in the higher echelons of the Admiralty.

James Burney was born in London on 13th June 1750, the son of musicologist Charles Burney and his first wife Esther. Very shortly after James' birth the family moved to King's Lynn, on account of Charles Burney's poor health. Once in Norfolk, Esther – who had nine children with Charles – gave birth to another child, the daughter Fanny who went on to become a famous novelist and diarist.

During this period in Norfolk the Burneys became acquainted with the Vancouver family. A few years separated James Burney and George Vancouver in age, though both would join the navy early in life and be presented with the opportunity to join Captain Cook's voyages to the Antarctic in the formative years of their careers.

*The family silhouette of James Burney.*

Their seagoing careers were to differ greatly: Vancouver was to achieve much but die young while Burney lived to a ripe old age but left a shallow imprint on maritime history. Despite eventually rising to the rank of rear admiral, Burney was not to leave the legacy that Vancouver did.

James Burney joined the Royal Navy in 1760 as captain's servant on the *Princess Amelia* which was part of the blockade of Brest, leaving Norfolk at about the same time that his family decided to return to live in London. He did well in his early years and was promoted to midshipman on the frigate *Aquilon* when he was 15.

He came home to England from India in 1770 at a time when all the naval talk was of Captain James Cook and his voyage of exploration. Within months of Cook returning from his first voyage (1768–71), plans were being made for a second great voyage that was to last from 1772 to 1775. Charles Burney used his friendship with John Montagu, the fourth Earl of Sandwich and First Lord of the Admiralty between 1771 and 1782, to secure James a position on board Cook's ship HMS *Resolution*.

He joined the vessel in December 1771 and sailed early the following year. Within a few months, in November 1772, he was promoted to second lieutenant on *Resolution*'s sister ship the *Adventure* under Tobias Furneaux after the first mate had to return home through illness. Throughout the expedition, Burney kept a detailed log and also drew charts. It was during this journey that Norfolk Island in the Pacific Ocean between Australia and New Zealand was named by Cook in honour of the Duchess of Norfolk.

Burney was also involved in one dramatic action at this time when called upon to lead a party of men to Grass Cove in Queen Charlotte Sound, New Zealand. They were to discover the bodies of 11 of their colleagues who had been slain by Maori. His name is recorded in this part of the world with Burneys Beach in Queen Charlotte Sound named after him. When the *Adventure* arrived back in Britain, Burney found a role as an interpreter to Omai, a Tahitian brought back to London. He was also charged with introducing the man to London society.

Before long, on appointment to second lieutenant on HMS *Cerberus*, he sailed to Boston in Massachusetts. However, with news of a further journey planned by

Captain Cook, Charles Burney again stepped in to use his influence to aid his son, a move which saw James summoned back to England to be ready to join Captain Cook's third voyage, to the Pacific.

Burney became first lieutenant on the *Discovery* under Charles Clerke and joined the ship which would sail with Cook's *Resolution* on February 10, 1776. With Clerke delayed, it fell to Burney to take the ship from the Thames to Plymouth where its commander finally joined them. The journey was ostensibly to return Omai to Tahiti but the principal purpose of the sailing was to attempt to discover the Northwest Passage.

Also on this expedition with Burney, in addition to Vancouver, was William Bligh, who would later captain the *Bounty* and its mutinous crew. Burney and Bligh became close associates as the journey of exploration continued.

In January 1778, Cook's ships discovered Hawaii and his crew became the first Europeans to visit, naming the archipelago the Sandwich Islands after the fourth Earl of Sandwich. It was on these islands, just over a year later on 14th February 1779, that Cook was murdered by a group of native inhabitants, an event witnessed by James Burney. That effectively saw the end of the expedition; the *Resolution* and the *Discovery* returned home. As the journey neared its end,

*A print showing Burney as a member of a group of influential men and women of his time. Burney is seated to the left of the right-hand table.*

*The* Resolution, *commanded by Cook, and the* Adventure, *with Burney on board, in Hawaii.*

Burney's immediate superior Captain Charles Clerke died, leaving Burney to bring the *Discovery* into the Thames.

Burney was later given command of HMS *Latona* to patrol the North Sea before being promoted post-captain in June 1782 on the 50-gun HMS *Bristol* with orders to escort 12 East India Company ships to Madras. At some point on the journey, however, Burney appears to have strayed from his specific orders, a decision that was to leave him out of favour with the Admiralty for virtually the remainder of his career. The *Bristol* took part in the battle with the French fleet in the Indian Ocean off Cuddalore on 20th June 1783 but later, whilst in India, Burney became seriously ill and was forced to return to Britain in 1784 without ever having the opportunity to redeem himself for his error of judgement. From there on, Burney went on the half pay list and his active naval career was effectively over.

In September 1785 he married Sally Payne (1759–1832) and they had three children, though one died as an infant. But his domestic life was less than orthodox and he left his wife in 1798 and went to live with his half-sister, the writer Sarah Harriet Burney (1772–1844), for five years before returning to his family. Later, he followed her lead and the success of his sister Fanny and developed a new career

*The young men of Norfolk who travelled, as Burney did, with the explorers must have been amazed at the sights and sounds of the Pacific islands. As their vessels nosed into the bays of places such as Hawaii, the forms of greeting would seem rather more threatening than welcoming. Violence did occur and Burney was present when Cook was killed. He might have been even more amazed at the way Hawaii looks today.*

for himself as a writer. His first project was to edit an edition of William Bligh's *A Voyage to the South Sea in HMS Bounty*, published in 1792, having been picked by his comrade from the Cook explorations specifically for the task. He went on to produce the five major volumes of his own work – *A Chronological History of the Discoveries in the South Seas or Pacific Ocean* – between 1803 and 1817 while remaining on the retired list of the Royal Navy. They were followed in 1819 by *A Chronological History of the North-Eastern Voyages of Discovery; and of the Early Eastern Navigations of the Russians*.

Living in James Street, Westminster, his new circle of friends were the leading literary and society names of the day: Samuel Johnson, Sir Joseph Banks and writers Charles Lamb, William Hazlitt and Robert Southey. Burney was elected a Fellow of the Royal Society in 1809. His handwritten nomination, finally dated 8th June 1809, read: 'Captain James Burney R.N., a gentleman well versed in nautical science and author of a History of Discoveries in the South Seas, being desirous of becoming a fellow of the Royal Society, we the undersigned do of our personal knowledge recommend him as worthy of that honour and likely to prove a valuable and useful member.' The signatories were: Jos. de Mendoza Rios; C. Blagden; M. Garthshore; H. Leigh Thomas; R. A. Salisbury; Anthony Carlisle.

At the time, his children were also enjoying professional and social success. Burney's son, Martin Charles Burney, became a barrister while his daughter married the Pall Mall bookseller John Thomas Payne. Intriguingly, Beethoven later dedicated a piece of music to Sarah Burney Payne in 1825, an allegretto quasi andante in G minor for piano.

The Burney family is also commemorated in the Burney Centre of McGill University in Montreal where the works of Charles, Fanny, James and Sarah Harriet Burney are catalogued. The centre is primarily dedicated to the publication of complete, definitive scholarly editions of the journals and letters of Frances 'Fanny' Burney (1752–1840) and the letters and memoirs of her father, the music historian Dr Charles Burney (1726–1814).

As the 19th century progressed, Captain James Burney had long since left his naval career behind though he remained on the navy retired list. As late in his life as July 1821, when still on that retired list, he was promoted rear admiral, primarily due to the intervention the Duke of Clarence (later William IV), who was Admiral of the Fleet. Four months later, on 17th November 1821, Rear Admiral James Burney was dead from a stroke. He is buried in St Margaret's church, Westminster.

# CHAPTER SIX

# John Fryer

## (1753–1817)

The mutiny aboard the *Bounty* is one of the most notorious episodes in British naval history. The names of those at the very centre of the damning chapter, Fletcher Christian and William Bligh, are synonymous with treachery and poor ship management and known even to those with only the slightest interest in matters maritime.

Yet this unfortunate episode also involved another key player, a man caught between the factions and carrying little favour with each as he sought to do his duty to his naval masters and his monarch. He was John Fryer, who was born at Wells on 15th August 1753.

Fryer grew up in the coastal town and married Ann Sporne in 1780, though within three years she had died. He was remarried in 1787, to Mary Tinkler, a few months after he had been appointed to the position of Master of the *Bounty* by the Admiralty on 26th August 1786. By the time he set sail, more than a year later and just two days before Christmas 1787, Mary was pregnant with his son Harrison, who was born in 1788. But he was not to see the infant until after the momentous events of the mutiny on the *Bounty*.

Even before the ship set sail for Tahiti, the seeds for a troubled voyage had already been sown. It was not a happy ship and the atmosphere aboard deteriorated further as the voyage progressed. When the mutiny finally erupted – on the morning of 28th April 1789 – the *Bounty* had been away from British shores for some 18 months and was fresh out of the paradise island of Tahiti, bound for a British slave colony.

The basic facts are believed to be that rogue elements of the 45-strong crew rose up against the captain, Lieutenant William Bligh, and seized the ship. However, there remains to this day a degree of mystery as to exactly what happened during this unfortunate naval episode and descendants of the key characters still argue over who the villains of the piece really were.

The omens for a peaceful crossing to Tahiti were bad from the outset: the ship assigned by the Admiralty for the task was already regarded by Bligh as inadequate, with an equally inadequate crew; there were no troops aboard to keep order; and the captain had little time for the Master, John Fryer. The two men failed to work well together and there was a degree of animosity. Bligh, it transpired, had favoured a friend of his family, Fletcher Christian, as the Master. However, unable to secure this position for Christian, Bligh instead made him Master's Mate.

Fletcher Christian, at 23, was strong and dark with a reputation as a ladies' man but also regarded as a slack disciplinarian. Not surprisingly, he was popular with the crew. Christian was the antithesis of Bligh, who was a man with a volatile temper but already with an established career in the Royal Navy, having served as

*Fryer's gravestone has been rescued from obscurity in the graveyard of Wells parish church and is safely placed in the porch. The Wells Local History Society provides an accompanying display and information and the place of his actual grave is now marked by a modern stone.*

master on HMS *Resolution* under Captain Cook before the explorer was killed on Hawaii in February 1779.

Bligh's repute as a navigator was exemplary. In fact his charts have been deemed so accurate that seamen are content to rely on them even now. His man management style, though, was another matter. During the outward voyage to Tahiti the relationship between Bligh and Christian had grown close, and the two men would often dine together.

The *Bounty*, formerly known as the *Bethia*, had been instructed to sail to obtain breadfruit and then ship them on to British colonies where they would be used as cheap food for the slave labourers. When the vessel arrived at Tahiti on 26th October 1788 it was akin to stepping ashore on a paradise island for the crew after the confinement of the ship. Beautiful beaches, a sub-tropical climate, plenty of fresh food and a warm welcome from the Tahitians awaited Bligh's

men. This was a lifestyle they quickly grew fond of and were equally loath to leave behind. While on Tahiti, the crew of the *Bounty* were permitted to relax, enjoy themselves and accept the hospitalities that were offered on the island.

Consequently, back aboard six months later, having acquired the breadfruit and awaiting the onward winds, life on the *Bounty* sat in stark contrast to that ashore on Tahiti. As with many issues surrounding the *Bounty* and the mutiny, it remains unclear exactly why the ship stayed on Tahiti for so long. But come the day of departure, all areas were crammed with the cargo of breadfruit plus coconuts which had been gathered for the crew's own consumption. The crew quarters were overcrowded and life became fraught and ill-tempered.

Bligh and Christian later clashed over this supply of coconuts, though the two men outwardly maintained their friendship. But eventually, the Master's Mate Christian – whose uncle, Rev. Humphrey Christian, was vicar of Docking in west Norfolk from 1766 to 1773 – had seemingly had enough and rebelled with elements of the crew, though no clear cut reason for the mutiny has ever thoroughly been explained.

The captain had no indication of the treachery that awaited him until the moment of the mutiny on that morning of 28th April 1789. The mutineers arrested Bligh, captured the ship and put him and some of his allies, who included John Fryer, into the ship's 23-foot launch and set them adrift.

Also in that boat was Fryer's cabin boy, 15-year-old Robert Tinkler, who was his brother-in-law. Tinkler later went on to be a renowned post captain and commander, wounded more than 20 times in various conflicts before he died, in the St Margaret's parish area of Norwich, in 1820.

Once adrift, Bligh managed to sail the launch more than 3,000 miles in seven weeks and back to friendly territory, eventually landing on Timor. Even on this small boat there was friction between Bligh and Fryer, who later revealed that his preference would have been to stay with the *Bounty* to try to recapture the vessel for the Admiralty.

While Fryer had remained loyal to his captain, Bligh showed little gratitude. He accused his Master of not doing enough to secure the ship or protect him when the mutineers took him from his stateroom located directly across from Fryer's cabin. Bligh later wrote of Fryer's role at the moment the mutinous crew struck: 'he saw them in my cabin, for our eyes met each other through his door window, and he had a pair of ship's pistols loaded and ammunition in his cabin'. Bligh commented that with firmer resolution, Fryer might have made good use of the weapons at his disposal. In his defence, Fryer argued that 'he could find nobody to act with' and as to the pistols, he said he was 'so flurried and surprised that he did not recollect them'.

Authorities on Fryer question the validity of this, pointing out there was no reference to this at the subsequent courts martial hearing. Within the deepening mysteries of the *Bounty* mutiny it is not inconceivable that the true version may have been clouded by people withholding information to protect themselves and others.

Once the small boat was cast off with Bligh, Fryer and the small contingent

*John Fryer*

aboard, Christian had taken command of the *Bounty* and sailed back to Tahiti, where some of the crew left the ship. These men were eventually captured and returned to England. Many were ordered to appear before a court martial hearing along with Bligh, who was cleared. Fryer gave evidence against the mutineers but did not testify against his captain. He never faced a court martial over the mutiny but those found guilty of the mutiny on the *Bounty* were hanged, no doubt dying with the regret that they did not remain with Fletcher Christian. He, with other crew members and Polynesians, sailed on from Tahiti and sought safe haven on the tiny Pitcairn Island in January 1790, where they settled.

Three years later, some of the mutineers, including Christian, were killed by the Polynesian men. But today, some of the island's inhabitants are direct descendants of the mutineers, speaking a dialect of Tahitian and 18th-century English.

The dramatic story of the British navy's most notorious mutiny has been retold many times in books and particularly in films where, in the true tradition of Hollywood, storylines have become blurred and key characters written out.

Fryer is a nautical figure whose reputation seems to have been tarnished by this one episode. He had an honest, hard-working and successful career apart from the period when he was involuntarily associated with Bligh. Once back in England, Fryer came back to Wells to be reunited with his family but it was not long before he was off to sea again to resume his career.

Before joining the *Bounty*, John Fryer had an eventful career. He saw action as an ordinary seaman in the 1770s and had been captured by the French who imprisoned him in Marseille jail for 15 months before he gained his freedom in a prisoner exchange and the right to fight another day. After the *Bounty* debacle, his career progressed again, despite Bligh's stubborn refusal to give his Master a reference.

Fryer went on to achieve the rank of post captain, excelling in his speciality of navigation and ship handling, and commanded several store ships including

HMS *Serrapis*, HMS *William* and HMS *Abundance*, as reward for his previous service.

Yet even before he secured his own command, other captains and admirals wrote about his conduct and the difficulties they would have encountered if they had not had Fryer's expertise to hand. Sir Hyde Parker, who was Admiral of the Fleet at the Battle of Copenhagen of 1801, specifically requested Fryer as his sailing master on the *Royal George* for the campaign. He took Fryer with him when he transferred to HMS *London*.

Captain Bligh also went on to continue his career and although he was involved in another mutiny – on HMS *Nore* in 1797 – he eventually attained the rank of vice admiral of the blue and died aged 64 in December 1817.

Fryer retired to Wells on 6th April 1812, after his health deteriorated, and died five years later on 25th May 1817, also aged 64. There is a plaque on the house in Gamble Square, where he died. With some careful detective work, local residents Mike Welland, Tom Sands and Alan Leventhall eventually located the grave's position thanks to an old photograph of the churchyard that had surfaced in Australia. Using this photograph and others of the churchyard, the location of

Fryer's grave was worked out and led them to a position where they found a stone lying face down with a distinct mason's mark on the back. Turning it over, the gravestone and final resting place of John Fryer was rediscovered. The original stone is now located in the church porch with a new stone laid on the spot in Wells churchyard bearing the inscription: 'This stone marks the grave of John Fryer R.N. 1753–1817, Sailing Master of His Majesty's Armed Vessel Bounty.'

# CHAPTER SEVEN

# *George Vancouver*

## (1757–1798)

Captain George Vancouver led what was arguably the longest mapping expedition in history. For the best part of five years, the Norfolk-born sailor mapped whole stretches of the west coast of America from northern Mexico to southern Alaska. To this day, islands, inlets, towns and cities bear his name. His legacy was immense in leaving charts and drawings that were so accurate that they were to benefit mariners for centuries after his premature death at the age of 40.

George Vancouver was born in King's Lynn of Dutch ancestry on 22nd June 1757, the son of the well connected assistant collector of customs at the port, John Jasper Vancouver. It was his father's links within the maritime community that enabled George's sailing career to be shaped so effectively from an early stage, for John Vancouver was able to secure for his son a coveted appointment on board Captain James Cook's ship, the *Resolution*, in 1772. This saw the young Vancouver sail away on the second of the explorer's three great voyages to the Pacific.

The position, much sought after, meant that Vancouver received a rigorous training in seamanship, navigation and surveying under Cook on a journey that took him as far as Australia and New Zealand.

When Cook's vessels returned safely to Britain in 1775, Vancouver had impressed to the extent that he was offered a place on the third voyage, which departed British shores in 1776 in search of the North-west Passage – a possible sea route through or around North America. Vancouver was joined on the mission by William Bligh and by the slightly older James Burney, also from King's Lynn and known to the Vancouver family. It was, however, a journey that was to have a fatal finale, Cook being killed by natives on Hawaii in February 1779.

Vancouver mourned the loss of Cook, but the premature ending of the expedition did little to hold back his flourishing career and he was to take all that he had gleaned from his experiences over several years of exploration with him onto his new postings. Upon his return to England later in 1779, Vancouver was commissioned as a lieutenant and served on HMS *Martin* and HMS *Europa*. He was also aboard HMS *Fame* in the victory over the French at the Battle of the Saintes of April 1782, which was fought out in the seaways between Guadeloupe and Dominica. He spent up to a decade with the West Indies fleet and charted many of the harbours in the Caribbean.

In his absence from England, the commercial world was changing, particularly with the international tensions that had developed along the American coastline. Russian fur hunters were advancing towards Alaska and British and American traders were gathering furs further along the coast. Amid this scramble for commercial and territorial dominance, Spain claimed sovereignty over the coast, although this was not recognised by Britain. The Spanish despatched an expedition to gauge the threat and in 1789 occupied Nootka Sound, later seizing three British ships that entered the harbour, a provocative move that brought Spain and Britain to the verge of war. At the time Vancouver was already being lined up to lead a major surveying expedition to those territories. A convention with Spain was eventually signed in October, ending the threat of war, but it still served to sharpen the focus of the assignment.

Vancouver received his command for the mission and was given three key tasks: to make a detailed survey of the coast from California to Alaska; to meet a Spanish commissioner at Nootka and settle the damage claims arising from the 1789 seizures; and to try to ascertain whether an entry to a North-west Passage, or a navigable passage that extended far inland, existed. In addition, he was to look for timber and minerals and fill in the gaps in the charts from Cook's final voyage.

Vancouver's ships, the 337-ton *Discovery* and the smaller *Chatham*, sailed from Falmouth on 1st April 1791, taking a route via the Cape of Good Hope, Australia and New Zealand before heading to the Sandwich Islands, now Hawaii. It would be years before he would return to Britain but it was a voyage that would see him established as one of the legendary chart makers.

Spending the summer seasons exploring as far north as possible and the winters in the warmer environs of Hawaii, the journey was often slow and arduous. Vancouver quickly made a number of significant discoveries including Puget Sound and later in June 1792 he became the first European to chart the inner waters of the Burrard Inlet, now the main harbour area of Vancouver city. The Norfolk mariner was meticulous in his work and not concerned that progress was often painfully slow as he plotted unmapped coastlines. He would often have his men row hundreds of miles inland to follow the true course of the land, taking endless lunar observations before setting out in order to calculate his exact position.

Vancouver later sailed for Nootka to meet the Spanish commissioner Juan Francisco de la Bodega y Quadra. They never successfully resolved the difficulties between their two countries but that did not prevent them from becoming good friends. As a record of that friendship Quadra asked

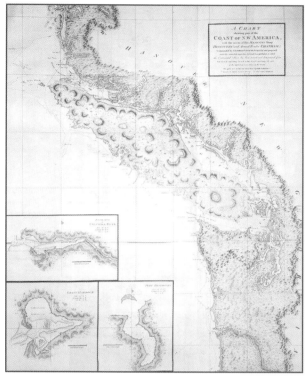

*Above: Vancouver's 'Chart shewing part of the coast of N. W. America', from* A Voyage of Discovery to the North Pacific Ocean and Round the World *(London, 1798). Below: etching from a sketch by Vancouver of Valparaiso harbour, Chile. The* Discovery *is anchored in the foreground.*

Vancouver to name 'some port or Island after us both'. Vancouver responded, declaring the spot where they met as Quadra and Vancouver's Island, though it has since been abbreviated to Vancouver Island. It was one of more than 400 place names bestowed by Vancouver in the course of his voyage, a high proportion of which still survive.

The spring of 1793 saw the ships back on the north-west coast, ready to resume their survey, though two crewmen were wounded in a rare attack on the expedition by Indians. The final survey season, in what is now Alaska, began in Cook Inlet and ended in a bay near the southern tip of Baranof Island in the Alexander Archipelago, which Vancouver named Port Conclusion. This was fitting, marking as it did the finale of one of the greatest ever maritime surveying ventures.

Despite the extent of the journey, which produced a series of charts still widely regarded as extremely accurate, Vancouver's 'plottings' did not chart the great rivers on the Pacific Coast, missing the Fraser River, Colombia river and the Skeena River. Some observers still express surprise at this, although closer examination of his orders show that he was clearly instructed 'not to pursue any inlet or river further than it shall appear to be navigable by vessels of such burthen as might safely navigate the Pacific Ocean'.

What Vancouver also established was that no North-west Passage existed at the latitudes that had been suggested. That discovery, and first navigation by sea, rested more than two centuries later with the Norwegian explorer Roald Amundsen in the period 1903–1906, though another Norfolk mariner, Samuel Gurney Cresswell, had already traversed the route over solid ice in 1852.

After a final call at Nootka, Vancouver's ships began the long voyage home after a voyage of exploration that had meticulously plotted some 1,700 miles of coastline. The *Discovery* arrived back in the Thames in October 1795. Since leaving Falmouth in 1791, the ships had sailed about 65,000 miles and its crews rowed another 10,000 miles in smaller vessels along uncharted inlets. Of the 180 men who sailed with the expedition, all but six returned safely, a remarkable achievement reflecting Vancouver's concern for the health and the welfare of his men. That safe arrival back on British soil brought to an end the longest mapping expedition in history.

Possibly Vancouver's greatest achievement was the charting work he carried out of the North-west and Pacific coasts of America. The conditions were changeable and arduous, the climate varying from the pleasant conditions around California to the harsher environment up towards the Alaskan panhandle.

Unfortunately for Vancouver, the expedition was not without its difficulties on board his vessel, most notably with a rogue member among his crew. A certain Thomas Pitt from a titled family was determined to create problems where he could, and once back in Britain he tried to use influence to sully his captain's name. Vancouver had Pitt flogged twice and eventually ordered him to leave the ship but the well-connected offender later criticised Vancouver publicly and even challenged him to a duel.

Yet Vancouver's name remains honoured across North America. Vancouver Island retains his name and while Quadra's has been dropped from the name of the island, there is a Quadra Street. There is also a Vancouver in Washington State, USA. The city of Vancouver, British Columbia, was named later by the chairman of the Canadian Pacific Railway. It stands on the site of an original wooden town called Graham, which burned down. When it was rebuilt as the railway arrived in the territory it formally became known as Vancouver, after the Norfolk seaman.

In the mid-1990s, the lack of a memorial to Captain George Vancouver in his own country or his home port began to cause a degree of unease among maritime enthusiasts. After a

*Two Vancouver memorials in King's Lynn: above, the modern statue by the Custom House; below: the Vancouver Centre – a place of trade is perhaps not inappropriate as a memorial.*

53

*George Vancouver*

meeting called in 1997, a number of people signed up to the cause to raise funds to erect a memorial to him in the form of a statue. Costing £28,000, it was unveiled in 2000 on the quay near the Custom House, King's Lynn. The communities of Vancouver BC and Vancouver, Washington, contributed and a plinth of granite from Squawmish near Vancouver, Canada, was imported to stand it on. In June 2007, there were further celebrations in Canada and Vancouver's home port of King's Lynn to mark the 250th anniversary of his birth.

Soon after his return to England in 1795, Vancouver retired to Petersham on the outskirts of London and he concentrated on writing up the account of his epic journey after the Admiralty instructed him to prepare his journal for publication. The published version, half a million words in length, was within a hundred pages of completion when Vancouver died on 12th May 1798, aged 40. His brother, John, ably completed the work.

Captain George Vancouver was buried in the churchyard of St Peter's at Petersham. A wreath from the mayor and council of the City of Vancouver is laid on the grave each year on the anniversary of his death and, appropriately, that city has arranged to have the grave cared for by the Petersham and Ham Sea Scout Group.

*The modern city of Vancouver in British Columbia, Canada, is perhaps the greatest memorial to the explorer. Cruise ships anchor alongside the exhibition centre, float planes land in the harbour and the city itself is a vibrant and attractive city.*

# CHAPTER EIGHT

# Tom Allen

## (1764–1838)

Few people were closer to Horatio Nelson than his body servant Tom Allen. Perhaps there was only one who knew the vice admiral better, his mistress and the mother of his daughter, Lady Emma Hamilton. But even that can be the subject of debate. While Lady Hamilton may have borne Nelson his beloved Horatia, Allen was the individual who catered for the sea lord's every whim while at sea. The two – the mistress and the servant – are, however, said to have got on well.

As Lord Nelson's personal servant, Allen was a constant appendage. Yet there remains a bizarre, even semi-tragic quirk, to their relationship. While Allen had been at Nelson's side throughout his illustrious career, fought with him in the great battles, shared his finest moments and tended him as he sustained serious wounds, he was strangely absent from Trafalgar. It poses the question: where was Allen when the sea lord needed him most?

What is without doubt is that he was tolerated by Nelson in a way that few other senior officers would have allowed. Allen was given more leeway than others would have done with their valet de chambre and he was permitted to offer opinion and advice above his station, a privilege not only tolerated but also encouraged by Nelson.

There was one particular attribute that Allen showed that Nelson valued highly, that of loyalty. It was this, combined with brutal honesty, that gave Allen a highly individual – possibly influential – role in Nelson's life.

The forthright and opinionated Allen was loathed by Nelson's contemporaries

© National Maritime Museum, Greenwich, London

*Tom Allen. It is rare to find such a portrait of the servants and sailors of Nelson's time.*

for his willingness to express his thoughts to those around him, often regardless of rank. Allen was a blunt-speaking Norfolk man, at times to the extent that he may even have embarrassed Nelson with that rural bluntness, particularly when Nelson was amongst peers who were not used to being spoken to in such a frank and familiar way by lower ranks.

But wherever Horatio Nelson ventured, the servant with a rough Norfolk accent was rarely far behind. Nelson was generally content to overlook this 'over-familiar' aspect of Allen's character and his shortcomings, acknowledging his broader contribution as an effective valet. The two also had another bond. They were both Norfolk men. Nelson undeniably favoured men from his native county and records show that among the 820-strong multinational crew aboard HMS *Victory* on 21st October 1805, there were at least 27 other Norfolk men.

Nelson hadn't needed to look far for Tom Allen. The two came from Burnham Thorpe, their lives inextricably linked by geography, values and perhaps common thought, while separated by an enormous class gulf. Yet there was respect on both sides. Nelson protected Allen, who was absolutely devoted to the vice admiral, and the two men worked well together; there was a unique bond. It was this, perhaps, that meant they so often stood side by side aboard ship in the heat of battle.

Allen was with Nelson at the Battle of Cape St Vincent (1797) and the Battle of the Nile (1798), manning one of *Vanguard*'s guns during the heat of the encounter. He was also present at the Battle of Copenhagen in 1801 and at Malta, where at one point he planted himself in front of Nelson to shield him from fire and razor-sharp splinters.

Allen never claimed to be a great sailor but he was present at, and indirectly contributed to in his own unique manner, the critical moments of Nelson's career. And that, per se, makes him important. But Allen was also absent from two significant incidents in Nelson's life: he remained aboard ship when Nelson lost his arm during the landing at Santa de Cruz, Tenerife, in 1797, and at Trafalgar the faithful servant quite literally missed the boat.

The blame for Allen missing Trafalgar may lie with master rather than servant. He was delayed in his departure from Burnham Thorpe to Portsmouth to join the 104-gun HMS *Victory* on Nelson's specific instruction. The vice admiral had asked that he stay behind to tie up various affairs before heading south. Less gallantly, there are suggestions that he may have been delayed en route south to join the ship by over-consumption of alcohol. The sources of this version, however, may well lie among those who did not favour Allen having such proximity and influence with Nelson.

Whatever the reason, what is beyond dispute is that by the time Allen did arrive in Portsmouth, the *Victory* had set sail. For Allen, the shame and distress of that stayed with him but there was also a point where it seemed that he would be disciplined too. The Admiralty wrote to him after Trafalgar saying that he was at fault and threatening him with a court martial, though the issue never reached that stage.

Allen felt deep pangs of guilt throughout the remainder of his life for his absence on 21st October 1805. He remained convinced that, if present, he would have been able to protect Nelson, not least in his own mind by persuading the vice admiral to wear different attire and thus become less conspicuous on the deck of his flagship.

Eyewitness accounts suggest Nelson would in fact have perished whatever he was wearing. His presence on the deck of HMS *Victory* would have been obscured by thick smoke and it is widely accepted that Horatio Nelson died from a chance bullet rather than a French sniper's pinpoint accuracy.

*Allen was with Nelson at the Battles of Cape St Vincent (depicted here), the Nile and Copenhagen, though not at Trafalgar.*

Tom Allen was born in 1764 and had been in the service of the Nelson family from his early years. He first went to sea with the naval hero in 1793, when Nelson was appointed captain of the *Agamemnon* after five frustrating years 'on the beach' in Norfolk, ashore and on half pay. He stayed with his master, even being given custody of his plate and jewels and charged with looking after Nelson when ill and nursing him back to health after being wounded.

Descendants of Tom Allen still live in Norfolk. With his wife Mary, he had a son, born in 1801, whom they named Horatio Nelson Allen. His daughter Susan (Tom's grand-daughter) was later raised by Tom and Mary. She married George Cushing, who was a tailor in Lobster Lane, Norwich.

Following Nelson's death, Tom Allen returned to Burnham Thorpe as manservant to Sir William Bolton, a relative of Nelson. But upon Sir William's death, Allen and his family fell upon hard times, regularly facing the threat of the workhouse. It was only in 1831 that life improved when he was admitted to the Royal Hospital at Greenwich as a pensioner, employed by the lieutenant governor of the hospital, Sir Jahleel Brenton, as a gardener. Promoted to 'pewterer' under the patronage of the now Rear Admiral Sir Thomas Hardy – 'kiss-me Hardy' of Trafalgar days and captain of the *Victory* in 1805 – he worked at the hospital until his death on 23rd November 1838.

Sir Jahleel communicated the event to Hardy with the words: 'It is with deep regret that I inform you that poor old Tom Allen is no more. He was taken off most suddenly and unexpectedly.'

*The public house at Burnham Thorpe, the village which both Horatio Nelson and Tom Allen called home.*

# CHAPTER NINE

# *George Manby*
## (1765–1854)

An eccentric genius, a failed soldier and an unfortunate sailor, yet George William Manby's legacy was to make the sea a safer place for mariners the world over. He was a prolific and persistent inventor, primarily focussing on devices that would save thousands of lives, particularly around the coastline of Great Britain in the early 19th century.

Because of his demeanour and manner, Manby was not widely liked or respected and rarely taken seriously in his own lifetime or in the years that followed his death. However, the lifesaving devices, apparatus and procedures he invented and pioneered continue to underpin rescue and safety at sea to this day. It should also be remembered that he was one of the early campaigners for an organisation that specifically focussed on the rescue of mariners in peril on the sea, the forerunner of the Royal National Lifeboat Institution.

He was the son of Matthew Pepper Manby, a captain in the Welch Fusiliers, and Mary Manby. He was born on 28th November 1765 at Denver Hall in west Norfolk, the eldest son of nine children; his family moved soon after that to Wood Hall at Hilgay. At the age of five he was sent to school at Downham Market where he always maintained that he was a great friend of an older boy at the school, one Horatio Nelson. Whether Nelson ever attended Downham Market School is the subject of debate among historians, the consensus being that Nelson was probably never a pupil there. Much of the evidence that he was, comes from Manby's own accounts and with Nelson being a little older than the inventor, it seems the two were unlikely to have met there. The story may have been part of the mythology Manby liked to build up around himself. Also, during the period Manby refers to, Nelson was more likely to have been at school in North Walsham and soon after that he would have been embarking on his own early sea career. What is beyond doubt is that Manby was a lifelong admirer of Lord Nelson, collecting items of Nelson memorabilia throughout and in his later days transforming his home at Great Yarmouth into a Nelson Museum.

After Manby completed his education at King's Lynn Grammar School, the family plan was that he should follow in his father's footsteps as a soldier but he showed little aptitude for that. He went to the Royal Military Academy at Woolwich in 1777 but in 1782 he was rejected for service in the American War because of his diminutive size and youth. Once, while home on leave, he did fire a mortar with a rope attached over the small tower at Downham Market Church – a precursor of what was to come.

In the years that followed, he spent his time writing pamphlets and historical works, and learning to sketch. Manby's early adult life was a fraught, unfortunate period. He spent some time in the Cambridge Militia before marrying the very attractive Jane Preston, daughter of the Rev Dr Preston of Waldringfield, Suffolk, in 1793. On his father's death, Manby inherited the family estate at Wood Hall but the couple were frivolous with the fortune and within five years it had all but gone. They were also hit by a flood which virtually destroyed their home in 1796.

They later moved to Wales where Jane started an illicit relationship with a Captain Pogson of the East India Company, leading to a vicious quarrel between the two men. In a brutal climax to the dispute, Manby was shot in the back of the head and though he survived he had to undergo an operation to remove the slugs. He recovered but suffered blinding headaches for the rest of his life. The broader circumstances surrounding the attack and its aftermath did little to ease Manby's problems and had a deep effect on his state of mind. Jane left soon after with Captain Pogson while, under pressure from his creditors, Manby was arrested for debt and placed in gaol.

It was his younger brother Thomas Manby (1769–1834) who was to come to his aid. Thomas was a captain in the Royal Navy and had served under George Vancouver on the *Discovery*, exploring the west coast of America. Manby Point in Alaska is named after him. He went on to enjoy a successful naval career, eventually rising to the rank of rear admiral before he became embroiled in a scandal that was centred on his relationship with Queen Caroline, the wife of King George IV. He later died of an opium overdose.

Thomas rescued George Manby from gaol and appointed him lay chaplain on the ship he commanded, the frigate HMS *Bordelais*, which had been captured

ship failed, thwarted in the jaws of the gale-force wind blowing onto the shore. Without this line, many of the ship's crew and passengers were trapped and subsequently perished in the bitter conditions.

As he watched the attempts to save them, a distressed Manby formulated the idea for apparatus that would save hundreds of lives at sea. His vision was for a device to fire a line from a gun to the ship in order to set up a link to the shore to carry out a rescue. Manby set to work on it the very next morning, using a mortar from Yarmouth Barracks for his experiments. Initial attempts failed for a variety of reasons: the heat of the explosion cut the rope where it was attached to the shot; soaking the rope in a cocktail of chemicals to stop it from burning also did not work; and using metal chains made it too heavy.

Manby endured the ridicule of the many spectators to his attempts. But he was persistent by nature. When he had an idea that he was convinced would work, and particularly if he believed that it would have real benefits to mankind, little would divert him from his task until he had found a way of making it work to his satisfaction.

After a series of attempts, and at the suggestion of a fellow officer from the barracks, Manby tried attaching the rope to the shot with a length of plaited leather and it held firm.

He gave his first public demonstration in August, just six months after the tragedy of the *Snipe* had so vividly unfolded before his eyes on that dark February night.

Before an audience of pilots, sailors and others interested in maritime safety, he used a five-and-a half inch brass mortar to fire a 24lb shot carrying a one-and-a-half inch rope 200 yards. It worked. The Suffolk Humane Society, which had supported the attempt, recognised this feat and awarded him a medal for his successful efforts in creating what became known as the 'Manby Mortar'. It was the first of many medals bestowed upon Captain George Manby for his work as an inventor.

The rope had been adapted with barbs that were designed to snag in the rigging of a ship in trouble. Once the device to send the line out to a stricken vessel was proven, the next element was to design a smaller vessel that could shuttle along the line to reach the crew and bring them to shore safely. For this purpose, Manby invented the 'unsinkable boat'. It seemed very much a makeshift solution and involved fitting wooden casks to the gunwales to act as buoyancy chambers, but it was effective. An indication of this is the response from local fishermen. Afraid that it would threaten their income from salvage work, they tried to sabotage the invention and jeopardise Manby's personal wellbeing.

On the night of 12th February 1808, Manby was presented with the opportunity to test his device after the brig *Elizabeth* was dismasted and ran aground on a sandbank. Manby roused his soldiers from the barracks to bring his mortar down to the beach. The line was shot out to the brig, hitting its target, and the 'unsinkable boat' hauled out to the vessel. Its grateful crew clambered aboard and were returned safely to the shore.

Over time, Manby refined the procedure. He fired a 'star shot' to illuminate the position of a vessel in trouble at night and also later invented a canvas sling in which a passenger or crew member could be placed and dragged along the rope via pulleys to the shore – a forerunner of the breeches buoy.

Manby had funded this work out of his own pocket thus far but later demonstrated the 'Manby Mortar' to a Parliamentary Committee which awarded him £2,000 to continue the work He was ordered to find suitable sites around the coast of Britain to erect his apparatus and identified 170 locations but it coincided with a change of government and tightening of budgets, and from then on little further money was provided to man and equip these stations. However, 59 stations were set up nationally with those in Norfolk and Suffolk proving particularly successful. By 1823, it was thought that 229 lives had been saved as a result.

The many devices Manby invented were wide ranging but generally had public safety and rescue in mind. Several are familiar items today. His next major invention was for saving people who had fallen through ice while skating. It included a noose held open with a whale bone to try to catch hold of people who were trapped. It invariably worked. Manby also designed the first portable fire extinguisher which was a copper cylinder containing water and chemicals and filled with compressed air. He also invented a 'jumping sheet' from which to catch people falling from heights in the event of fire. Another proposal was that lighthouses should each have a unique signal, rather than emit a steady beam of light. It is a system still in use today. He also impressed the Admiralty with a gun which fired by percussion with the shells exploding on impact.

On one of his adventures, he travelled aboard the whaling ship *Baffin* to the Arctic to try out another invention not dissimilar in principle to the line developed to rescue people from stricken ships – the harpoon gun.

In 1814 Manby's estranged wife Jane died and he remarried. His second wife was the shy and submissive baronet's daughter, Sophia Gooch. But with his growing list of inventions requiring more of his time, he was rarely at home and spent weeks travelling around the country promoting his devices. As was typical of Manby, he was still also living way beyond his means and accruing large debts.

Manby had one other brilliant idea – that of forming a society specifically concerned with saving life from shipwrecks. In 1824 he helped found a Royal Society for the Preservation of Life from Shipwreck, supported by the Archbishop of Canterbury and Sir William Hillary. It was later to become the Royal National Lifeboat Institution, with Sir William Hillary, who had spent much of his fortune providing lifeboats and equipment, becoming regarded as its founder rather than the eccentric Norfolk inventor. His name was honoured, however, in 1829 with the Great Yarmouth and Gorleston Lifeboat named the *Manby*.

Poor luck dogged Manby, despite his election as a Fellow of the Royal Society in 1831. He was given little credit for his work and his ideas, despite their obvious success and benefits to maritime safety. Always in debt, he gained very little personal fortune from his schemes – which more often than not did work as planned. He was, however, awarded a large number of medals in recognition and he liked to wear them at every opportunity. He was obsessively attached to them. Little hurt him more than when they were temporarily seized for non-payment of a bill.

His second wife, Sophia, died in 1843 and in the latter part of his life Manby began to suffer ill health. At the age of 80, he was dismissed from his post at the

*A coastguard team mans a Manby mortar. Mortars such as this were sited all round the British coast and much further afield; examples can be found at North American museums as well as in the Time and Tide museum at Great Yarmouth. They continued in use until replaced by more effective and accurate rockets.*

barracks and retired to a small home in Gorleston, which he later converted into a Nelson Museum, taking the basement as his own living quarters.

It was there that he died aged 88, on 18th November 1854. He left his head to the Norfolk surgeon Sir Astley Cooper while the rest of his remains were buried close to his parents in the churchyard at Hilgay.

Despite the array of medals for his efforts, there was little financial reward or the public fame he craved, to accompany these honours. The knighthood that he had so coveted for such a large part of his life, and thought he deserved, was never forthcoming.

Yet Manby's contribution to maritime safety was immense. A marble tablet in Hilgay Church best sums this up, bearing the inscription: 'In the churchyard near this spot rest the bones of George William Manby, F.R.S. A name to be remembered as long as there can be a stranded ship.'

*Manby's house in Gorleston; he had a small museum here in honour of Nelson and gave the impression, incorrectly, that he knew Nelson from school at Downham Market. There is a display about Manby and a splendid oil painting of him in the Time and Tide museum at Great Yarmouth.*

# CHAPTER TEN

# *Sir Edward Berry*

## (1768–1831)

It may seem a somewhat unfair question to ask of a man who was one of the heroic captains of Trafalgar, but was Captain Edward Berry really one of Norfolk's greatest sailors, or was he just plain lucky?

Few seamen of the immediate post-Nelson era were more decorated or were more fortunate in the line of fire than Captain Berry. He sustained wounds that were serious enough to leave their mark and earn praise for gallantry but not to halt a promising career as he picked up medals on several major campaigns, serving in close proximity to Nelson at the Battle of Cape St Vincent and the Battle of the Nile before his role at Trafalgar.

This was the backdrop for Berry's career as he navigated a consistently upward path through the rank structure of the British Navy. Nelson respected and admired Berry, even referring to him as his 'right hand' though at some stage the vice admiral did become aware that Berry was not quite the completed article of a captain that he needed him to be. Brave, loyal and fortunate, even something of a lucky omen he may have been, but Berry lacked the outstanding seamanship skills displayed by many of his contemporaries.

In *The Command of the Ocean: a Naval History of Britain 1649–1815*, N. A. M. Rodger sums up Berry's career more brutally as 'a catalogue of gallant bungling interspersed with longer and longer periods of unemployment'. Yet he rose to the rank of rear admiral and in the years after Trafalgar there was only one other person in the whole of the British Navy who had as many medals as Berry and that was Admiral Cuthbert Collingwood, the man who succeeded to command of the British fleet at Trafalgar upon Nelson's demise.

Berry's early rise to stardom owed much to the support and patronage of Horatio Nelson, but even Lord Nelson eventually had to acknowledge Berry's limitations.

Born in 1768, Edward Berry was the son of a London merchant but his father died when he was still young. The family were left in financial difficulties and Edward was educated from an early age under the patronage of his uncle, Rev. Titus Berry, at Norwich Grammar School.

Young Berry entered the Navy as a volunteer aboard HMS *Burford*, possibly when he was only ten years old. But luck was with him from that early age. As Signal Midshipman on HMS *Duke*, he almost lost his life when a shot flew close enough across him to knock him senseless. That he was gallant is undeniable and his courage was rewarded with advancement. He was promoted for his bravery in boarding vessels and in May 1796 became first lieutenant to the then Captain Horatio Nelson on HMS *Agamemnon*, the vessel that in 1793 had given Horatio a return to sea after his five years marooned on half pay 'on the beach' in north Norfolk.

By the time of the Battle of Cape St Vincent in February 1797, Berry was a Commander but officially only a passenger aboard Nelson's ship HMS *Captain* and had no particular duty on board. However, when there was a fight, Berry was not one to stand idly by. When Nelson laid HMS *Captain* alongside the Spanish ship *San Nicolas* and gave the order for boarders, Berry was the first man over the side. His actions were also noted by the commander at St Vincent, Admiral Sir John Jervis, who described him in a report to the Admiralty as 'an officer of talents, great courage and laudable ambition'.

Nelson's fame grew considerably from the success at Cape St Vincent and in that October he was knighted. He chose as his companion for that occasion Edward Berry, a sign that the two men were now firm friends. At the ceremony, when King George III remarked upon the loss of his right arm, Nelson gestured to Berry and wittily replied: 'But not my right hand, your majesty, as I have the honour of presenting Captain Berry.'

By that stage, it had been agreed between them that Berry – who was engaged to be married – was to be Nelson's next flag captain. With rumours of French plans to occupy Egypt, Nelson wrote to his younger protégé in late 1797 with the following advice: 'If you mean to marry, I would recommend your doing it speedily, or the to-be Mrs Berry will have very little of your company.'

On 12th December Berry married his cousin Louisa Forster, daughter of Dr Samuel Forster, the headmaster of Norwich Grammar School. A week later he

*Two sketches of Berry survive amongst contemporary pictures.*

was formally appointed as flag captain of HMS *Vanguard*. The appointment was to place Berry at the heart of the emphatic defeat of the French at the Battle of the Nile on 1st August 1798 at Aboukir Bay, though the journey out to the Nile was at times perilous and seemed to expose Berry's shortcomings. When the *Vanguard* was dismasted in a gale on the journey to the Mediterranean, the finger of blame pointed in the direction of Berry.

Yet his courage and actions at the height of the battle were beyond question. It was also Berry who caught the semi-conscious Nelson after he had been hit by a flying fragment and suffered a head wound. Nelson was so fearful he uttered to Berry: 'I am killed. Remember me to my wife.'

Later Nelson was to thank Berry for his contribution at the Nile with the words: 'I shall never forget your support for my mind on the 1st of August.' But after the battle, Berry was sent back to Britain in the *Leander* carrying Nelson's dispatches, while Thomas Hardy took over as flag captain on *Vanguard*. Nelson, it seemed, now had a new 'right hand'.

Berry's limitations were clearly exposed when set against the superior seamanship qualities of Thomas Hardy, who would later captain HMS *Victory* at Trafalgar and be a future First Sea Lord. Nelson had already recognised his qualities and made the decision that his young protégé was not the man to have by his side at the most critical of moments. In Hardy, Lord Nelson had found a man of immense capability.

Frustratingly, on his return to England, Berry was engaged en route by one of only two French ships to escape the Nile confrontation, the *Généreux*. He was also wounded during the melee, hit on the arm by a flying fragment of another man's skull. He eventually arrived in England in December where news of the Nile victory was already known. But he was feted as a hero, knighted and granted the Freedom of the City of London and lauded in Norwich, his home city.

Oddly, Berry found this an irritation as well as a pleasure. Upon his return to Norwich, he wrote:

> the people received me with mad joy. In short, I'm so great a man that I'm very in and out everywhere to the great annoyance of my pocket and distress of my feelings.

Early in the spring of 1799 Berry was appointed to the HMS *Foudroyant* and directed to assist in the blockade of Malta. This provided an unexpected opportunity for revenge and to complete the rout of the Nile when he was able to capture the 74-gun *Généreux* in February 1800 in what was his finest hour. Soon after, he took the *Guillaume Tell*, which had also fled the scene at Aboukir Bay.

Such was his joy that he immediately sent the giant ensign from the *Généreux* home to Norwich as a gift to city mayor Robert Harvey. For many years the flag was displayed alongside a portrait of Nelson in the city's Blackfriars Hall and then moved to the castle keep where it was last seen in public in 1905. It still exists in the ownership of Norwich City Council. In 2005, members of Norfolk Heraldry Society lobbied for the flag to be put on display for the Trafalgar bicentenary celebrations but the council insisted the flag was too fragile and too big to place on public display, with restoration costs put at £340,000.

Berry's fame, however, was short-lived. A few months after the capture of the French warship he returned to England to experience the same fate that befell his great patron Nelson in 1788 – left without a ship for around five years. Berry felt slighted by the Admiralty, angry and frustrated. He fretted as he saw his standing in the service diminish, despite support from Nelson who sympathised with Berry's predicament. But in the summer of 1805, it was a trusty old vessel that came to the rescue. He was appointed captain of the *Agamemnon*, the same vessel that had rescued Nelson's career from oblivion.

Oliver Warner notes in *A Portrait of Lord Nelson*:

> It was typical of Berry's luck that, having long and restlessly awaited a new ship, he should have been given the *Agamemnon*, before having the infinite happiness of joining Nelson on the eve of his greatest battle.

Berry fought at Trafalgar as one of Nelson's 'band of brothers', and despite the Vice Admiral's reservations of Berry as a great seaman, he was confident enough in his ability to have him close by at Trafalgar. When Berry joined the fleet with *Agamemnon* on 13th October 1805, Nelson reportedly exclaimed: 'Here comes Berry! Now we shall have a battle.'

Berry was regarded as a lucky charm to such an extent that Captain Henry Blackwood on HMS *Euryalus* remarked: 'Berry is such a bird of good fortune, that now he is arrived I feel that the enemy will make a bolt.'

At Trafalgar, as the battle raged, Berry had to bide his time. It was almost two in the afternoon when HMS *Agamemnon* joined the fray, sailing alongside HMS *Neptune* and HMS *Conqueror* to bombard the Spanish battleship *Santissima Trinidad* into surrender. In the end, Berry's contribution was as an extra fighter more than as a skilled tactician, though maritime historians tend to agree it was his leadership and seamanship that was questionable, never his bravery. Captain Edward Codrington of the *Orion* – in the line next to the *Agamemnon* – noted that during the battle Berry was blazing away for all he was worth 'at friend and foe alike'.

The bond of friendship that had evolved between Berry and Nelson never waned and as the battle was being won, he felt deep and fearful concern for his mentor. Agitated by the thought, Captain Berry had himself rowed across to HMS *Victory*, sensing all was not well on board the flagship. However, by the

*Berry is one of the 'band of brothers' pictured studying the plan for the Battle of Trafalgar.*

time he arrived, his patron and friend Horatio Nelson was already dead.

In 1806 Berry was created a baronet, taking the title Sir Edward Berry of Catton in honour of the village near Norwich he had an affinity with and where he lived for some time in The Warren at Old Catton. Now demolished, it is said that the garden was laid out in the pattern of a ship's quarterdeck.

His record was exceptional. He was the only officer in the Royal Navy at the time, except for Collingwood, to have had three medals, having commanded a line-of-battle ship in the battles of the Nile, Trafalgar and San Domingo against the French in 1806. But his fighting days were effectively over. After commanding *Sceptre* and *Barfleur* he was placed in charge of one of the royal yachts in 1813. Despite appeals to the Admiralty, he was given no further important postings. Appointed rear admiral of the blue in 1821, later rear admiral of the red, he suffered poor health for the remainder of his naval career and died heirless in Bath on 13th February 1831. He is buried at St Swithin's church, Walcot, Bath. A plaque on the church wall records his deeds:

> The distinguished services of Sir Edward Berry, are recorded in the annals of his country. He was the friend and companion of Lord Nelson, under whose command he fought at the battle of St Vincent, The Nile and Trafalgar; he commanded HM Ship *Agamemnon* at the Battle of St Domingo, and was honoured by his sovereign with three medals, for great naval victories.

Lucky or not, Captain Sir Edward Berry has a record that speaks for itself.

*Cape St Vincent. In the seas off here, Berry led the boarders from HMS* Captain *onto the* San Nicolas.

# CHAPTER ELEVEN

# *Sir William Hoste*

## (1780–1828)

Wherever you delve into Norfolk's maritime history, the ghost of Vice-Admiral Horatio Nelson is rarely far away. There are uncountable connections between him and other mariners, ships or locations.

Nelson was a leader who was quick to recognise the need to encourage and support members of his crew, to ensure they were adequately fed, cared for and clothed. He was also one to offer help, advice and patronage to friends and acquaintances who he felt were worthy or deserved to progress in the Royal Navy. If such acquaintances were men of Norfolk, then the support they received was often substantial.

One such fellow who benefited from Lord Nelson's patronage was William Hoste. He went on to become an accomplished naval captain and he never forgot this support. Indeed, in what was to be his most perilous, yet finest, hour he drew on the strength of his association with Lord Nelson to see him and his crew through to victory and safety.

As is well-documented, Nelson was proud of his Norfolk roots and known to hand pick as many of his crew from Norfolk as he could. Hoste, it appears, was paramount amongst the favoured and the suggestion is that he may also have been protected at the critical moment. Like Nelson, Sir William Hoste was the son of a Norfolk clergyman who went to sea and found fame.

Born on 26th August 1780 at Ingoldisthorpe, he was the son of Dixon Hoste who was rector of Godwick and Tittleshall in Norfolk. The priest was a tenant of Thomas William Coke (1754–1842), who later became the 1st earl of Leicester at

*School House at the Paston School (later to become Paston Sixth Form College), North Walsham. On the right is the classroom where both Nelson and Hoste were educated. The Nelson Room contains primarily recollections of the older man, but Hoste is not forgotten.*

Holkham Hall. Hoste was educated at Paston School at North Walsham – where Nelson was taught for a period.

It was through Coke that Dixon Hoste obtained an introduction to Nelson and as a direct consequence of that, his son's first adventure aboard came with Nelson's reappointment to a British warship in 1793. By late January 1793, after the latest reminder to the Admiralty that he was anxious to serve, Nelson knew that he was to get the ship *Agamemnon*, a vessel his crew unflatteringly referred to as 'Eggs and Bacon'.

A few months later, in April 1793, William Hoste entered the British navy as a captain's servant, under the special care of Nelson, who was overjoyed to be back at sea after his uncomfortable and frustrating five years 'on the beach' in Norfolk. To crew his ship, Nelson turned to many of the Norfolk men he knew and trusted. There were newcomers too, including Hoste and another Norfolk clergyman's son, John Weatherhead. Within the year, Hoste was promoted midshipman and when Nelson transferred to HMS *Captain* in 1796, Hoste moved with him, to fight at the Battle of Cape St Vincent.

Understandably, Hoste admired Nelson immensely. He respected, perhaps even adored, his great mentor. In the years that followed, the pupil was able to see on many occasions the courage of Nelson, and never more vividly than when he lost his right arm at Tenerife in July 1797. At the time, Hoste was serving aboard the *Theseus* as a midshipman and it was to this vessel that Nelson was taken after suffering the wound. His protégé was a witness to the operation to amputate the arm and recalled Nelson's courage: 'He underwent the operation with the same firmness and courage that have always marked his character.'

Hoste, having risen to the rank of lieutenant, was still aboard the *Theseus* at the Battle of the Nile. Following that devastating defeat of the French, and still only 18, he was appointed captain of the brig *Mutine*. He held the position for three years and in 1802 was appointed post captain by Lord St Vincent, who as Admiral Sir John Jervis had been in overall command at the Battle of Cape St Vincent in February 1797.

Ill health dogged him over the next couple of years after he contracted malaria in Alexandria but by the end of 1804 he was again operating along the African coast in command of HMS *Eurydice*. Nelson undoubtedly helped guide Hoste's progress in the Navy and may well have recognised some of his own traits in the young seaman as he offered encouragement and patronage.

Sir William Hoste's career developed steadily up to 1805, when Nelson appointed him to command the *Amphion* after one of his other senior officers was invalided home. But Hoste only served briefly with Nelson in September 1805, strangely missing Trafalgar as a result of the Vice Admiral sending him off on a diplomatic mission to Algiers. There is speculation as to why, though it is only speculation: Nelson had already lost two of his other promising protégés:

HMS Agamemnon, Captain, Vanguard, Elephant *and* Victory – *a picture published in 1808 to recall Nelson's ships, but also the ships of some of the men featured in this book.*

*Captain, later Sir William, Hoste.*

John Weatherhead, the son of Rev. Thomas Weatherhead of Sedgeford, was killed in Tenerife while Edward Parker was severely injured and died in 1801.

Did Nelson send his surviving 'student', a fellow Norfolkman, away for fear that he would become embroiled in the Battle of Trafalgar and be killed? Or is it mere coincidence? The truth remains a mystery.

Hoste deeply regretted not being involved at Trafalgar and, like all who had benefited from Nelson's wisdom and support, was devastated when he learned of the Vice Admiral's death several weeks later. He spent the following years of his active naval career in the Mediterranean and the Adriatic. His role was to secure British trade interests in the area with navy vessels involved in blockade, commerce protection and attack missions. It was a task he accomplished with aplomb and ingenuity.

From 1808 to 1814 he commanded a force of frigates engaged in operations against the French around the Dalmatian coast, often fighting a French squadron that had been formed under Napoleon's orders at Venice. Hoste was regarded as competent in his task and the work was lucrative with prizes gained from captured Italian and Dalmatian merchant ships. It is estimated the Norfolkman pocketed a handsome £60,000 from these exploits, a significant fortune in those early years of the 19th century. Hoste is also credited with successful attacks on French military sites on shore.

Yet what he is best renowned for are his exploits on 13th March 1811 in command of HMS *Amphion*. A Franco-Venetian squadron of six frigates and around five smaller vessels with 2,000 men aboard attacked Hoste's force of four frigates near the island of Lissa. The French Commodore Bernard Dubourdieu attempted to imitate Nelson's attack at Trafalgar.

Perilously outnumbered and potentially outgunned – Hoste had 124 guns manned by 900 men to Dubourdieu's 276 guns – Hoste drew on the strength of Nelson to inspire his men. Recalling the patronage his mentor had shown him during his early career, he hoisted the signal 'Remember Nelson', and flew it from *Amphion*'s masthead as the enemy ships closed.

The French commander sailed down on the English with his ships in two

*Sir William Hoste is commemorated by this memorial in St Margaret's church in King's Lynn.*

lines but Hoste proved too smart and with rapid manoeuvres and expert gunnery outwitted the French. Dubourdieu was killed, a French frigate driven ashore and two of the Venetian vessels were taken. British losses were 50 dead, 132 wounded. *Amphion* was badly damaged in the ensuing combat and was forced to return to England where Hoste was given command of HMS *Bacchante* with 38 guns.

The exploits off Lissa attracted a great deal of attention in England, shifting the balance of power on the Dalmatian coast while also earning Hoste lasting fame. Hoste's name is commemorated both here in Norfolk and at the site of his most famous achievement, Lissa (now known as Vis): a small island nearby is named Hoste Island. Bizarrely, the Croatian islanders have more recently founded the William Hoste Cricket Club in his memory. The move recalls games organised by Hoste during the British occupation of the territory and follows the emergence of a letter he wrote to his mother during the Napoleonic wars 200 years ago. As British naval commander of the Adriatic station for about three years, he encouraged his seamen to play cricket to stave off boredom and in the letter home he extolled the island's virtues as a cricketing venue. 'We have established a cricket club and when we anchor for a few hours it passes away the time quite wonderfully,' he told his mother.

Closer to home, the question is whether one of Norfolk's most famous hostelries, the Hoste Arms, is named after Sir William Hoste. That is less clear. Built in 1550, the building was originally the manor house of Burnham Westgate with records first showing it as an inn or hotel in 1651. Owned by the Pitt family, it was named the Pitt Arms and became the first coaching stop on the route from Wells to London. Nelson was known to have visited the inn during his lengthy stay ashore in Norfolk between 1788 and 1793. There are two suggestions as to how the popular hotel and restaurant obtained its current name, though the name change in 1811 does curiously coincide with Sir William's greatest success at sea.

While nostalgia may favour the decision as one which honoured Sir William's success off Lissa, the second, and more practical explanation, may simply be a case of land ownership. The Hoste family were huge landowners in the area and had recently acquired Sandringham and more land in the Burnham area. That there is such a connection with Hoste remains appropriate. Hoste was an accomplished seaman, a fine frigate captain and was possibly the most talented of Nelson's followers.

Made a baronet in 1814 and knighted in 1815, he married Lady Harriet Walpole in 1817. His last major appointment was in 1825 to the royal yacht *Royal Sovereign*.

Illness curtailed Hoste's career and he died on 6th December 1828, a father of three sons and three daughters. He is buried in St John's Chapel, London.

# CHAPTER TWELVE

# *William Lukin*

## (1768–1833)

As a 74-gun vessel of the line, the *Mars* created a fine sight as it moored off Cromer on the rather drizzly summer afternoon of 31st July 1807. It was a scene that happened to fall into the view of one of Norfolk's great artists, John Sell Cotman, who was a young, up-and-coming painter, though perhaps more preoccupied at the time with courting his future wife Ann Miles, the daughter of a tenant farmer from the Felbrigg estate. That view, of warships lying sedately at anchor off the Norfolk coast with the *Mars* at their midst, led to one of his best-known watercolours, *The Mars off Cromer*.

The captain of the vessel during that period was William Lukin, a solid and reliable naval commander who lived at Wells and through a fortuitous set of genealogical circumstances would eventually inherit Felbrigg Hall.

William Lukin was born on 20th September 1768, the son of Rev. George Lukin who was rector of Felbrigg and Aylmerton, just next to Cromer. He first went to sea probably as early as 1781, when he was a mere boy of 13. He appears to have learned well, kept his head down at the appropriate moments and survived in the harsh climate aboard ship. In 1786 he was a midshipman on the *Expedition*, by 1793 he had achieved the rank of Lieutenant and 1795 saw him in command of the sloop *Hornet*, ahead of his promotion to post captain. That promotion gave him command of the *Thames*, a vessel of 32 guns, and saw him rise steadily within the navy as Britain faced war against France.

Lukin was fortunate in having a powerful patron in William Windham III, the squire of Felbrigg who would eventually make the young man his heir.

*The Mars off Cromer: painting by John Sell Cotman.*

*Felbrigg Hall at the end of the nineteenth century. Today it is a National Trust property.*

back to north Norfolk with the plan to find a small estate to retire to, farm and bide his time until he inherited Felbrigg. He settled on the estate at Metton, close to Felbrigg, farming and shaping his ideas of how he would improve, expand and transform Felbrigg when the time came.

With his wife Anne, they had 13 children – and only one died in infancy. Consequently, with six sons and six daughters to raise, the family finances were stretched. In an attempt to cut their expenses they decide to move abroad and spent 1820–21 living in Brussels, but they were back in Norfolk when Cecilia Windham died on 5th May 1824, with Admiral Lukin - now 56 – not only assuming the estate but also taking the name and arms of Windham.

He began the alterations to Felbrigg he had been planning for so long with vigour, having already engaged the architect W. J. Donthorn to draw up extravagant extensions that would have virtually doubled the size of the existing house. This included a vast new dining room, a grand double staircase, offices and a new stable block. The stable block was eventually added, in redbrick for economy, but nothing else was done.

Lukin's eldest son William Howe Windham would succeed to the estate; of his other sons, George and Henry were destined for the navy, Charles for the army, Robert for the law and Joseph for the church. Establishing them in their respective professions proved expensive and there were the six daughters to consider as well.

Felbrigg Hall still stands on its National Trust-owned estate in north Norfolk.

*As commander of the defences of the north Norfolk coast, Lukin would have had overall responsibility for the Fencibles, seen here on parade at Cromer on the west cliff top.*

It is an impressive and well proportioned building, but it could quite easily have taken on a very different appearance in the early years of the 19th century if Lukin had been able to secure the funds to have his own way with the building and the estate.

A Whig by tradition, he left the politics to his eldest son who became MP for East Norfolk. Few letters and documents detailing the latter years of Vice Admiral Lukin's life have survived and he appears to have taken little part in public or local life, leading a peaceful and uneventful existence as a country gentleman until his death on 12th January 1833 aged 64.

# CHAPTER THIRTEEN

# *Sir William Bolton*

## (1777–1830)

A critical factor in advancement within the Royal Navy of the late 18th and early 19th centuries was the support of a wealthy and influential patron. Without such support from a family member, well connected friend or associate, a naval career could quite easily find itself becalmed.

Lord Nelson benefited immensely from the patronage of his uncles Maurice and William Suckling, though even he found his career in the doldrums in the late 1780s and was left without a ship for five years. When Nelson's career did resume, he turned patron and mentor and several of the men he chose were from similar backgrounds to his own as the son of a village parson: William Hoste and John Weatherhead were both young men of that ilk. William Bolton was another 'son of a village parson' who was to enjoy Nelson's patronage, though in his case there was additional advantage of being a relative. Born in 1777, William was the son of Rev. William Bolton who was brother to Nelson's brother-in-law Thomas Bolton, who had married Nelson's elder sister Susannah (1755–1818). The young William Bolton was also later to marry Nelson's niece Catherine.

Thomas Bolton, a corn merchant from Wells, and Susannah lived at Thorpe near Norwich after they were married before moving to Bolton House at Burnham Thorpe. It was at this time, in 1788, that William first met Horatio Nelson, who stayed with his sister and brother-in-law for a while after marrying Fanny Nisbet and returning from Nevis in the West Indies. So William Bolton was already well known to Nelson when he took him on as a 'captain's servant' on the *Agamemnon*.

*Bolton was at Nelson's side at the Battle of St Vincent, one of the four great sea battles which raised Nelson to the status of national hero.*

It is from this period of near constant combat for Nelson that his young protégés Edward Berry, William Hoste, Edward Parker, John Weatherhead and William Bolton were to benefit. While Parker and Weatherhead suffered premature deaths, Hoste, Berry and to a lesser extent Bolton were to go on to much greater achievements in the Royal Navy.

Nelson's patronage of Bolton during his early years at sea was crucial. Between 1793 and 1797, he was never far from Nelson who in turn was never far from the heart of the action. Bolton's early career is the story of Nelson's career as it flourished.

The 64-gun *Agamemnon* set sail for the Mediterranean and by October 1793 had seen its first significant action in running down a French convoy. Captain Nelson was seemingly pleased with his protégés and wrote to his brother, Rev. William Nelson of Hilborough near Swaffham, 'Hoste is a very good boy indeed, as is Bolton.'

Also aboard the *Agamemnon* was Josiah Nisbet, the son of Nelson's wife from her first marriage.

Bolton was aboard in 1794 as the *Agamemnon* besieged the French coast and also assaulted the town of Calvi, where Nelson was to lose the sight in his right eye after being hit in the face by splinters thrown up from a shell. The *Agamemnon* was involved in various attacks and skirmishes but by 1796 was part of the fleet of Sir John Jervis, who had been appointed commander-in-chief of the Mediterranean station. Soon after, Nelson transferred to HMS *Captain*, taking midshipman Bolton with him, and by early 1797

*Bolton was a junior officer on the* Theseus *with Nelson for the abortive attack on Santa Cruz de Tenerife. A visit to the harbour today can include seeing a panorama of the attack and the cannon which is reputed to have fired the shot which injured Nelson's arm.*

was in pursuit of the Spanish fleet. This pursuit culminated in the Battle of Cape St Vincent with Nelson and his crew performing heroics against the enemy vessels. For his role, Nelson was knighted.

Nelson took over the *Theseus*, taking Hoste and Bolton with him, later losing his arm in the attack at Santa Cruz de Tenerife. Nelson returned to the UK to recover from his wound, while William Bolton remained on the *Theseus* having been promoted lieutenant despite only having served four of the six years usually required for such promotion.

As Nelson's career developed, Bolton remained at his side, following the now rear admiral Nelson to the *Vanguard* and the *Foudroyant* and serving at the Battle of the Nile of 1798. When Nelson left the ship in Naples in 1800 to accompany Lady Emma Hamilton back to the UK overland through Europe, William Bolton sailed back on the ship to England under Captain Berry and in 1800 was involved in the famous capture of the *Généreux* and the *Guillaume Tell*, the two French ships that had escaped relatively unscathed from the Battle of the Nile two years earlier.

By 1801, after the Battle of Copenhagen, William Bolton was appointed commander of the 30-gun sloop *Dart*, where he stayed until she was decommissioned the following year.

Nelson still clearly thought very highly of Bolton and demonstrated that most visibly in 1803 when he was to be invested as Knight of the Most Honourable Order of Bath at Westminster. However, three days before the ceremony was due to take place, Nelson was appointed Commander-in-Chief of the Mediterranean Fleet. Reluctant to cancel the investiture, he appointed Captain William Bolton to represent him. Not only was Bolton to be Nelson's proxy, he was to be knighted as well.

On 18th May 1803 he became Sir William before proceeding to his wedding ceremony to marry Nelson's first cousin Catherine Bolton and, the following day, in the Princes Chamber standing in for Viscount Nelson as the Duke of York conferred Nelson's knighthood. Sir William and Catherine's first child, a daughter born in 1804, was duly named Emma Horatia.

Soon after, under Nelson's influence, Bolton was appointed master and commander of the sloop *Childers* with responsibility for carrying letters from the Prime Minister to Nelson at his station in the Mediterranean. He was later deployed on intelligence-gathering missions.

Throughout this period, Nelson seemed content with Bolton's seamanship but concerned at his lack of 'prize money'. Writing to Lady Hamilton, he said: 'Bolton does very well in his Brig but hasn't made a farthing in prize money.' Later, in November 1804, Nelson engineered an opportunity to bring a change of luck for Bolton and made that explicit in a letter to Lady Hamilton in November:

> Sir William Bolton is just arrived from Malta. I am preparing to send him a cruise, where he will have the best chance I can give him of making ten thousand pounds.

Bolton was successful but Nelson remained concerned that he was not accruing as much prize money as the opportunities he gave him merited. Despite this, Nelson saw his relative appointed to the recently-captured Spanish frigate *Amphirite* and confirmed post rank captain on 10th April 1805, to be sent to the Mediterranean as flag captain to Sir John Knight, the port admiral at Gibraltar.

Bolton was not at the Battle of Trafalgar but joined Admiral Collingwood's fleet two days later on 23rd October as captain of the *Eurydice*. In the years that followed, he operated off the Spanish and Irish coast aboard the *Druid, Endymion* and the *Forth* before it returned to Chatham in 1816 where it was decommissioned. Between 1818 and 1824 Bolton was left without a ship on the Navy's half-pay list as his career came to a close.

Bolton returned to Burnham Thorpe and took in Tom Allen, Nelson's manservant, after the Vice Admiral's death at Trafalgar. Captain Sir William Bolton continued to live in Norfolk until his death on 16th December 1830.

# CHAPTER FOURTEEN

# James Sharman

## (1785–1867)

Able Seaman James Sharman was one of thousands of men press-ganged into the fleets of the Royal Navy of the late 18th century. As a boy of 14 he had been a stable lad at the Wrestlers Inn at Great Yarmouth when he had the King's shilling foisted upon him and was taken by the press gang in 1799.

The Wrestlers Inn, since rebuilt, was the hostelry famously used by Nelson when he arrived in the port in November 1800 with an entourage that consisted of Sir William and Lady Hamilton, her mother Mrs Cadogan, her friend Cornelia Knight, Tom Allen and an Egyptian maid named Fatima.

Sharman's unplanned entry into the Royal Navy was eventually to see him aboard HMS *Victory* at the Battle of Trafalgar. Until that point, he had served on a number of vessels and joined the crew of HMS *Victory* in 1803. Able Seaman Sharman, or Sherman as he was occasionally known, is clearly listed on the ship's muster at the time of Trafalgar. He was close to Nelson in the Vice Admiral's final hour and it was he, assisted by Marine Sergeant James Secker (who was from Norwich) and another sailor, who are said to have helped carry the mortally wounded Nelson below deck.

In a bizarre twist, rather than this being the end of Sharman's association with Lord Nelson, it was in fact the beginning of a link he was to retain for the rest of his life.

Sharman served on various vessels after Trafalgar but when he later returned to Great Yarmouth, he found a job as 'keeper' of the Nelson Memorial, or as it was officially known the Norfolk Naval Pillar.

The Memorial, on South Denes Road, is one of the great landmarks of the town. A campaign to erect a memorial was launched in 1814 when a group of Norfolk businessmen formed a committee to raise funds. Within a year,

*HMS Victory afloat in Portsmouth: from a glass lantern slide dating probably from the 1880s.*

£7,000 had been collected and the search was initiated for an architect and an appropriate design. The committee eventually settled on an Athenian Doric column by London-based architect William Wilkin – who was also a Norfolk man, originally from Norwich. It was chosen from 44 proposals. The first stone was laid on the South Denes on 15th August 1817 by the Honourable Colonel John Wodehouse. The area, at the time, was an open area of grassland between the beach and the river Yare. The Nelson Monument was completed in 1819, is 144 feet high and bears the figure of Britannia looking inland towards Nelson's birthplace at Burnham Thorpe. On the western side of the pedestal is a Latin inscription, part of which reads:

This great man Norfolk boasts her own, not only as born there of a respectable family, and as there having received his early education, but her own also in talents, manners and mind.

The glory of so great a name, though sure long to outlive all monuments of brass and stone, his fellow countrymen of Norfolk have resolved to commemorate by this column, erected by their joint contributions.

The final cost was about £9,500 because deeper and stronger foundations were needed. It also funded a custodian's house next to the monument. There were specific conditions as to who should occupy the abode and become the keeper, with the property described as 'a cottage for a sailor to reside in, and to shew the monument: one who has fought under the banner of the Immortal Hero is intended to be selected'. Able Seaman Sharman was duly picked as the 'keeper', quite probably by Captain Thomas Hardy, and it was a job he kept for the rest of his life.

*This print of the Norfolk Nelson pillar also purports to show Peggotty's hut, with Sharman supposed to be the inspiration for Dickens' Peggotty.*

For Sharman, who was born in Yarmouth in 1785, life was far from uneventful. In 1827, he was said to have performed heroics during the rescue of a crew from the brig *Hammond*, a feat that was to bring him fame and acclaim beyond his wildest imagination and see him later immortalised in one of the great literary works of the 19th century. When Charles Dickens read the newspaper reports of the event, he was anxious to meet the former seaman. He arranged a visit to Yarmouth, staying at the Royal Hotel, and went to see Sharman in his cottage. With parts of *David Copperfield* set in Yarmouth, Dickens based his character

Ham Peggotty on Sharman, turning the press-ganged sailor into a minor celebrity for years thereafter.

Sharman, who had a daughter, still has descendants living in Norfolk. The census of 1861 shows him in residence in the keeper's cottage on South Denes Road at the time and aged 75. He had been an enthusiastic custodian of the monument, delighted to show visitors around and regale them with first-hand tales of Trafalgar and Nelson from the days of HMS *Victory*. He'd gladly accept tips and the praise and admiration from visitors, including Nelson's daughter Horatia who is said to have given him five shillings and a bottle of wine. For many, he was a colourful character, a living link with the dramatic victory at the battle of 1805. Heavily bearded and a large man, he was often seen wearing his medals including the Naval General Service Medal.

He died in 1867 at the age of 82 and is buried in Yarmouth.

*James Sharman wearing his Trafalgar medal.*

CHAPTER FIFTEEN

# Nelson's men at Trafalgar

In the cramped conditions of the 104-gun HMS *Victory*, a crew of 820 men lived, slept, ate and fought. It was a truly multinational crew: with a core of about 700 sailors from England, Scotland, Ireland and Wales, there were some 120 men of 18 other nationalities from as far away as Brazil, Canada, India, Malta, Norway and Portugal. There were also 146 marines on board.

Within that crew were 27 of Norfolk's finest. It is more than coincidence that this core of the crew should have its origins in Vice Admiral Horatio Nelson's home county. He favoured men of Norfolk, felt he could rely upon them and as a Norfolk man through and through, felt comfortable with seamen from Norwich, Yarmouth, the Burnhams, Attlebridge and King's Lynn beside him.

Nelson is famed for proclaiming in 1800: 'I am a Norfolk man and glory in being so.' What he is also reported to have said during his career as Britain's greatest naval hero is 'one Norfolk man is as good as any two other', which underlines suggestions that he seemed to recruit actively from the county.

At Trafalgar, HMS *Victory* suffered casualties: 102 injured with 57 dead, including Vice Admiral Horatio Nelson. There were further casualties among the Norfolk contingent. Jasper Berry, 21, from St John's, Norwich, George Kennedy, 22, from Rougham and James Mansell, 25, died alongside 47-year-old Nelson. John Bush, at 21, was described as dangerously wounded with splinters in every part of his body. But he survived and died on Christmas Eve 1845 in Greenwich Hospital.

Overall, 624 British sailors and Marines lost their lives at Trafalgar with a further 1,402 wounded. Casualties on the French and Spanish side were much higher at 7,300 killed or wounded.

Many Norfolkmen aboard HMS *Victory* and other ships of the British Trafalgar fleet survived to tell the tale. They included Ordinary Seaman Thomas Leverick, 20, Landsman John Whitton, 23, and his 22-year-old brother Thomas who was a crew's carpenter. All escaped uninjured. Yarmouth men John Thorling, 46, who was the quartermaster, and marine private Charles Nicholls also came away from Trafalgar unscathed.

There were Norfolk connections elsewhere among Nelson's Trafalgar ships which took on the combined French and Spanish fleet. Of the 18,000-strong multinational crews of the British ships at Trafalgar – just under one fifth of the entire navy at that time – around 280 of the men who fought alongside Horatio Nelson shared a common bond with their leader that they were all men of Norfolk and more specifically, that 71 came from Norwich.

About one in six of them were 'press-ganged', others at Trafalgar were volunteers anxious to serve their country in its hour of need, while a further group

*Paintings of the death of Nelson carry through the relationship between Nelson and his men by ensuring that many of the sailors are featured.*

*The names of Nelson's men have become better known since 2005, when both the National Archives and a private project made available the full list of the crews at Trafalgar. Pictures, however, are rare; these are sketches of men who served at the Battle of the Nile.*

were officers hoping for a glorious naval career that aspired to the heights of the heroic vice admiral who commanded them.

Whatever their station, these were men who lived life in the most challenging and dangerous of conditions with the threat of disease, sickness, injury or punishment on ships notoriously high. In battle, there was the danger of being on a crowded gundeck with razor sharp splinters scything the air. Living, eating, sleeping and working in close quarters, often for months at a time, were an everyday hazard for men of the line. Meal rations included a pound of ship's biscuit or hard tack, 2lb of salted pork or 2lb of salted beef on four days of the week. On other days it may have been cheese. In addition they'd get two pints

*Mr Rivers is one of the known faces in the sketches.*

of dried peas, three pints of oatmeal, seven pounds of bread and six ounces of butter plus porridge and occasionally fruit and vegetables. To drink, there was foul water and a daily ration of a gallon of beer and rum.

Holding a key position on another of the Trafalgar ships was the sailing master of the *Temeraire*, George Brackenbury from Norfolk. With a sister 98-gunner, *Neptune*, alongside and *Victory* ahead, this triumvirate of ships formed the spearhead of the British attack.

Others were Able Seaman Henry Hawes, from Norwich, who joined the HMS *Royal Sovereign* in 1803 aged 34 as a volunteer. He was wounded at Trafalgar and received a Parliamentary Award of £4 12s 6d and prize money of £1 17s 8d.

Ordinary Seaman John Plattern, a man of 'middle stature' and the son of William and Nancy Plattern from Walsingham, joined the HMS *Bellerophon* in November 1804 and was wounded at the battle, receiving prize money and a pension of £12 for three years. He sustained gunshot wounds and an ankle injury which left him 'very much disabled' and saw him discharged from service.

William Pilch from Burnham had joined the navy at 14 and was a Volunteer First Class. Serving on the *Bellerophon*, he was awarded the Naval General Service Medal and lived until 1863 when he died in Broadstairs, Kent.

In comparison Midshipman Merrick Lloyd from Bawdeswell from the *Sirius*, the son of Richard and Elizabeth, was granted £10 14s 2d prize money but this was never claimed. Wounded, he died in Malta Hospital on 23rd April 1806, aged 20.

Over half of the crew members were in their twenties and there were 274 boys aged between 10 and 14. Fewer than one in ten of the men were over 40. At 47, Nelson was one of the oldest, though 22 years younger than Walter Burke, the purser of the *Victory*, who was 69. He survived the battle, living another ten years after Trafalgar.

# CHAPTER SIXTEEN

# Samuel Gurney Cresswell

## (1827–1867)

In traversing the fabled North-west Passage, Samuel Gurney Cresswell made one of the great maritime discoveries. He had been part of rescue missions that had searched the ice for the ships and crews of an expedition that had previously attempted to seek out the sea route that linked the Atlantic and Pacific Oceans. But when the discovery finally came for Cresswell, it was not at the culmination of a great exploratory quest, but more at the end of an incredible feat of survival across some of the most challenging and arduous terrain on earth.

In the annals of great Norfolk seafarers, the name Samuel Gurney Cresswell is not one that readily springs to mind. He is frequently, and in many ways not surprisingly, overshadowed by those larger-than-life characters of Vancouver, Shovell, Myngs and Narborough let alone Horatio Nelson himself. Cresswell also had the misfortune to die relatively young. But he was the first naval officer known to traverse the entire North-west Passage linking the Atlantic and Pacific oceans via the Canadian Arctic Islands – and survive. At the time, this was a monumental feat and of great significance.

Historically, the North-west Passage has been ice-bound throughout the year, but with climate change the ice cover has been steadily shrinking and recent summer reductions have now made the sea route – the most direct shipping route from Europe to Asia – fully navigable for the first time since official monitoring began in 1978. That thaw sparked an international dispute: Canada said it had full rights over the North-west Passage in its territory and that it could bar transit through, while the US and European Union disputed this and argued that the

*Samuel Gurney Cresswell.*

new route should be an international strait that any vessel can use.

This route, trail-blazed by a Norfolk man, was discovered towards the middle of the 19th century. The North-west Passage, linking the Bering Strait to Hudson's Bay and Greenland, had for many years been identified as a possible alternative to traditional trade routes that at the time were controlled by empires opposed to British interests.

This route had been – it emerged later – discovered by Sir John Franklin and his ships *Erebus* and *Terror*, though after passing through Baffin Bay neither Franklin nor his crew were ever seen again. Between 1848 and 1853 two expeditions searched for the lost expedition and Samuel Gurney Cresswell, from North Runcton near King's Lynn, enthusiastically volunteered to join them.

He had joined the navy in 1842, when he was 14, serving aboard Sir Thomas Cochrane's flagship HMS *Agincourt* in the China Seas and rising to the rank of lieutenant.

This was a swashbuckling time – Cochrane was a renowned sailor and believed to be the inspiration for the exploits of Horatio Hornblower in the novels by C. S. Forester. The young Cresswell also distinguished himself in action against pirates near Borneo and Brunei.

While Cresswell was serving with distinction in warmer climes, Sir John Franklin was leading an expedition in search of the North-west Passage. He sailed from Greenhithe on 19th May 1845 with 129 officers and men aboard the *Erebus* and *Terror*. The expedition was well funded, both ships being fitted with the latest navigational equipment. But in the frozen wastes of the Arctic they disappeared, last seen moored to an iceberg in Lancaster Sound towards the end of July.

In 1848, a first mission was launched to try to find Franklin. Cresswell volunteered to join the *Investigator*. When he returned in November 1849, Cresswell had no hesitation in joining a second voyage to find out what had happened to Franklin and his crew. HMS *Investigator* was now under the command of Captain Robert McClure (1807–73). As in the first voyage, this second found no trace of Franklin, his ship or his crew, but what it did eventually produce was the first recorded crossing of the Passage.

It was remarkable, however, as much for its epic escape and the resolve and resilience of the men who made that journey. The *Investigator* sailed from Britain around Cape Horn, up the western coast of the Americas and through the Bering Strait to begin its second search from the Pacific side of the northern Canadian coast. The *Investigator* searched but with little success and then eventually became trapped in ice in Mercy Bay on the northern coast of Banks Island on 25th September 1851.

With a crew on the verge of starvation, having spent more than 18 months trapped in the ice, hope of rescue finally – and unexpectedly – arrived on 7th April 1853, in the person of Lieutenant Bedford Pim, who brought information that two ships commanded by Captain Kellett were berthed near Melville Island.

McClure despatched Creswell with six of the sickest crew members over the hazardous ice routes to the rescue ships some 160 miles away. The North Runcton man, it was reported, conducted his mission with efficiency and no loss of life. From there, he was sent further east to Beechey Island with more sick men and with despatches for the Admiralty. In the bleak, icy wilderness, in what was barely more than a stroke of incredible good luck, they encountered HMS *Phoenix*, which took them back to Scotland. Samuel Gurney Cresswell was duly credited with being the first person to traverse the North-west Passage. It was also the first complete circumnavigation of the American continent. McClure was knighted for his leadership in the expedition.

It was an epic journey in itself, on sled, on foot and by boat, finally delivering word to an empire that had spent three and a half centuries in search of a northern sea route connecting the Atlantic and Pacific oceans.

Creswell had enjoyed the patronage of an influential friend and champion in the Arctic explorer, Rear Admiral Sir William Edward Parry (1790–1855). Parry, who it is suggested secured Cresswell's position on McClure's voyage, was not slow in publicising his protégé's achievement. In a detailed letter to *The Times* in November 1853, he methodically outlined how Creswell and his party had left the *Investigator* for Kellett's ships and was then ordered further onto Beechey Island and a passage home to break the news in England.

He revealed that Creswell had taken four weeks to cover that second 300-mile leg of the journey, leaving the Arctic on the *Phoenix* on 23rd August and arriving at Thurso in the far north of Scotland on 4th October. Parry ends his letter:

Fifty-three hours' travelling brought them to London. On Friday, October 7th they arrived at the Admiralty with tidings that the geographical

*The* Investigator *amid the ice, searching for evidence of Franklin and his men.*

question of the long sought for Northwest Passage had been satisfactorily solved.

What Cresswell was able to announce was that Franklin had succeeded, albeit at cost of his life and that of his crew. A few years later, it was confirmed that Franklin's ships had all but completed the navigation of the North-west Passage, and Franklin was entitled to the honour of its discovery.

Just over half a century later, in 1906, the Norwegian explorer Roald Amundsen successfully navigated the route by sea, although his voyage via the Rae Strait was through young ice and shallow water. That suggested that although it was possible to navigate the route by sea, it was not at that time likely to prove to be commercially practical.

Cresswell was related to the Gurneys of Norwich through his maternal grandmother the prison reformer Elizabeth Fry, but it was one of his latter-day descendants, the former BBC Economics Editor Dominick Harrod, who was more recently to bring his name to a wider audience.

In the early 1990s, Harrod made a chance discovery of a canvas bag in the home of his mother, Lady Harrod, the widow of the distinguished academic and economist Sir Roy Harrod, at the Old Rectory at Holt. It was full of sketches and letters Cresswell had written to his parents in King's Lynn, each labelled Baltic, Arctic or China. Mr Harrod found them compelling reading and edited and introduced them in his book *War, Ice, Piracy: The Remarkable Career of a Victorian Sailor*.

As well as being a competent sailor, Cresswell was also a capable artist and from his epic journey he was able to produce a vivid set of sketches that added a splendid dimension to his account of this incredible escape and discovery of the North-west Passage. Copies of the sketches were soon proving popular. A tiny advertisement in *The Times* of 15th February 1854, for example, briefly related Cresswell's part in the discovery of the North-west Passage and added:

> From sketches he had taken during the voyage, eight have been selected for publication. The views will be printed in coloured tints, on paper 18 inches by 25 inches and will be enclosed in a stiff paper wrapper. Price £2 2s. the set.

Cresswell was feted for his role in the great discovery. On 26th October 1853, King's Lynn welcomed him home with a lavish banquet in the Assembly Rooms where the Town Clerk read a congratulatory address and the Mayor, Lionel Self, presented him with a copy on an illuminated scroll on vellum to which the seal was attached by a golden cord. On that occasion, Cresswell regaled the audience with some of the hardships which he had suffered whilst leading his sledging party across the ice.

> We used to travel all night, about 10 hours, and then encamp, light our spirits of wine, put our small kettle on it to thaw the snow water, and after we had our supper – just a piece of pemmican and a glass of water – we were very glad to get in, after smoking our pipes.
>
> The first thing we did after pitching the tent was to lay a sort of macintosh cloth over the snow. On this would be a piece of buffalo robe stretched. Each man and officer had a blanket sewed up in the form of a bag, and this we used to jump into, much the same as you may see a boy in a sack. We lay down, head and feet, the next person having his feet to my head, and his head to my feet, just the same as herrings in a barrel. After this we covered ourselves with skins over the whole of us, and the closer we got the better, as there was more warmth.

From 1854, Cresswell served as a commander with the Baltic fleet in the war against Russia before sailing to China in the Chinese war on the Peiho River. In September 1859, he was promoted to full captain, but his naval career was curtailed by his failing health.

The polar ice epics are a key part of Cresswell's story in a 20-year naval career but it was the rigours of the Arctic winters that were eventually to cut short his life. Samuel Gurney Cresswell died at the age of 39 on 14th August 1867. His funeral was held on 22nd August and his gravestone stands in North Runcton churchyard.

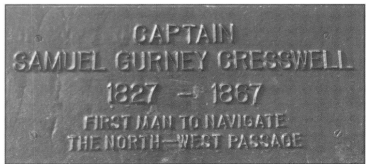

*Cresswell is now amongst those Norfolk mariners recognised on the plaques in the compass by the Purfleet at King's Lynn.*

# CHAPTER SEVENTEEN

# Lord Fisher of Kilverstone

## (1841–1920)

First Sea Lord John 'Jacky' Fisher of Kilverstone was a figure of immense importance in reforming the Royal Navy, a mariner who played a critical role in shaping the British navy and naval warfare for the 20th century. There are, however, differing views over the manner he went about those reforms and whether he was as effective as he had hoped to be, particularly in assembling a deterrent force. Some regard him as a senior admiral who is up there with Nelson in the impact he had on the history of the British Royal Navy, while others assess him as vain and ruthless, a man who took on his rivals and made himself unpopular in some circles.

He was, undeniably, a determined naval reformer and a man who left a colossal legacy. Considered far-sighted in his reforms, which revolutionised the navy, he is credited with simultaneously triggering an arms race as he strove both to avoid conflict and to change the face of warfare at sea.

It is hardly accurate to describe Fisher as a 'great sailor' because despite rising to the highest naval office in the land as First Sea Lord – on not one but two occasions – he built his career on achievements as a shore-based officer rather than a seafarer. Unusually, he felt happier on dry land. He acknowledged that fact, conceding, in his own words: 'To be a good admiral, a man does not need to be a good sailor. That's a common mistake. He needs good sailors under him.'

As a forceful and progressive-thinking reformer, it was he who took the navy from an age of wooden sailing ships and coal-powered vessels into the Dreadnought era of big guns and fast oil-powered warships. A renowned gunnery and torpedo expert, what Fisher – later Baron Fisher of Kilverstone in Norfolk - did was to transform the Royal Navy into an efficient, modern fleet, equipped with the finest warships on earth.

He knew all about wooden sailing ships. His career started at a time when the Royal Navy still had many actively in operation but his service was to span 60 years and end with the fearsome *Dreadnought* and the introduction of submarine warfare. Despite this creation of a navy with awesome firepower, Fisher had a natural loathing of war and his efforts were primarily geared towards preventing conflict and defending the assets of the British Empire as they were.

John Arbuthnot Fisher was born the eldest of 11 children on 25th January 1841 in Ceylon, now Sri Lanka. His father was Captain William Fisher, a British army officer with the 78th Highlanders, and was aide-de-camp to the governor of Ceylon. He joined the Royal Navy aged 13 on 12th June 1854, at Portsmouth with HMS *Victory* as his first ship. He served on a number

*Fisher served on HMS* Warrior, *now restored and on display in Portsmouth. Whilst never engaged in significant action,* Warrior *marks the transition from the 'wooden walls', the great sailing ships: she had a full set of sails, but was the first all-iron sea-going armoured battleship.*

*By the end of his career, Fisher had guided the navy from sail power through coal as a fuel to the use of oil and into the age of the 'dreadnought' battleships.*

Hall and the estate near Thetford in south Norfolk had been given to Fisher's son Cecil by the Admiral's close friend Josiah Vavasseur who was a director of the Armstrong Whitworth company.

Lord Fisher retired in January 1910 but retained a keen interest in naval affairs. The powerful British navy he had created had not acted as the deterrent to war in the way he had envisaged, and Winston Churchill persuaded him to come out of retirement and become First Sea Lord to replace Prince Louis of Battenberg, who left office because of his Germanic connections. But there soon appeared cracks in the relationship with Churchill, who was the First Lord of the Admiralty, primarily over the Dardanelles expedition. Fisher eventually resigned over the campaign on 15th May 1915, complaining that it involved the misuse of spare Admiralty vessels. He served out the remainder of the war at the Board of Innovations. The dispute also affected Churchill's career and led to him resigning as First Lord of the Admiralty and spending time in the political wilderness.

Fisher's family remain adamant that Jacky Fisher made a priceless contribution to the Royal Navy and Britain's national security and that his effort, vision and commitment was vital in modernising the fleet before World War 1 and during it. History, though, does appear to have been kind to Jacky Fisher – concentrating on his achievements rather than his character.

Lord Fisher died in 1920, aged 79, after a battle with cancer and is buried in the churchyard at Kilverstone.

# CHAPTER EIGHTEEN

# Sir Arthur Knyvet Wilson

## (1842–1921)

For a naval man, Sir Arthur Knyvet Wilson won his Victoria Cross in the most unlikely of settings. Having seen limited combat in more than a quarter of a century of military service, the Royal Navy officer – then a 41-year-old captain in the Naval Brigade – found himself in the midst of a deadly skirmish more than ten miles away from the ocean in the eastern deserts of Sudan.

It was unexpected, as Wilson had joined the morning's expedition as 'loafer', someone who'd merely gone along to witness the fight rather than find himself at the heart of a bloody melee. But as the discipline of the British advance slipped, the experienced captain was suddenly thrust into the centre of the fray and at close quarters with a dangerous enemy.

The uncertainty of such a rapid turn of events required decisiveness, courage, clarity of thought and action. That Wilson was to display all of those virtues not only led to a successful outcome and avoided another embarrassing setback for the British, but also led to his award of the nation's highest military honour for bravery, the Victoria Cross. Thereafter, Wilson was feted as a local hero in his home town, received national acclaim and saw his career head off on a trajectory that would take him to the highest naval office in the land.

Arthur Knyvet Wilson was born in Swaffham on 4th March 1842 into a family with an established military history. His father was Rear Admiral George Knyvet Wilson and his mother Agnes Mary. He was the nephew of Major General Sir Archdale Wilson of Delhi, who was later to be embroiled in the Indian Mutiny of 1857–58 and the siege of Delhi, which rocked British control of India to the

*A picture book graphic showing Wilson gaining his Victoria Cross.*

core. There was also a long ancestral lineage that linked the Knyvet-Wilsons to royalty. An old Etonian, Sir Arthur could trace his lineage back to the youngest son of Edward III and had blood ties with Edmund Knyvet, Sergeant Porter to Henry VIII.

Joining the navy straight from school, by the age of 16 he had already seen action at sea as a young midshipman in the Crimean War and the China War of 1858, but his career coincided with a rare period of peace between the major powers of the day and he saw no further action until the Egyptian campaign of 1882.

A torpedo expert, by 1884 Wilson was in Malta in command of HMS *Hecla*, a torpedo depot ship attached to the Mediterranean fleet. From there, he was despatched to the Sudan with a naval detachment of 240 marines and seamen. Wilson had arrived at the Red Sea port of Trinkitat in February 1884 in support of the Sudan campaign. The Mahdi was rebelling against the Anglo-Egyptian rule, which had thrown large parts of Sudan into turmoil, and events had taken a serious turn for the worse when the prominent slave trader Osman Digna had backed the Mahdi and was besieging garrisons at Sinkat and Tokar.

Facing humiliation from a number of embarrassing setbacks, the British Army decided that a show of force was required in the region. Wilson's men joined a force of about 4,000 under the command of Major General Sir Gerald Graham who were to advance inland to take a small fort and then move to the village of El Teb, where the rebels had scored their latest victory. Wilson's contingent brought with them three Gatling guns and three Gardner guns.

Wilson's role with the advancing party was vague. There was not even a specific requirement that he accompany the armed men. But he decided to join them, as little more than a spectator, in the hope of seeing some action. On 29th February 1884 at the Battle of El Teb, Graham's men advanced in the traditional 'square' formation. Aided by artillery pieces, they enjoyed initial success in keeping the Arab forces at bay, and pushed further forward, but their formation began to disintegrate as small groups of troops pushed enthusiastically ahead in an ill-disciplined form towards a line of trenches. Spotting the smaller groups that were becoming isolated from the main formation, the rebels seized their moment and broke out of their trenches, braving the bullets of the advancing British troops, and attacked the advancing line in close combat fighting with spears and swords. The courage and ferocity of the advance surprised the normally well disciplined British forces and the ensuing chaos placed the whole offensive in jeopardy.

During the advance, Captain Wilson had attached himself to the right half-battery of the Naval Brigade in place of a lieutenant who had been severely injured. During the Arab charge, the enemy seized one of the detachment's guns as the British were forced into rapid retreat, pursued by the enemy with swords and spears. In the fray, Wilson found himself projected forward from the relative safety of the centre of the 'square' to the front of the line and into single combat with the enemy.

Hand-to-hand fighting ensued and while most of the Sudanese were soon cut down by bullets a courageous contingent continued to advance into the retreating British infantry. As Wilson later wrote, they 'came on without the slightest fear', turning him from casual spectator into the hero of the Battle at El Teb.

What followed next can best be described in Captain Wilson's own words:

One fellow got in close to me and made a dig with his spear at the soldier on my left. He failed to reach him, and left his whole side exposed, so that I had a cool prod at him. He seemed to be beastly hard, and my sword broke against his ribs. The man on my right was a plucky fellow, and collared him around the neck and tried to throw him. The Arab still held onto his spear, so I hacked at him in a futile kind of way with the stump of my sword, and while I was doing so a second Arab came up and hit me over the head with a sword. My pith helmet took the greater part of the blow, so it only just cut the scalp and I hardly felt it.

The close combat continued for several minutes until men of the 1st Battalion, York and Lancaster Regiment, came to his assistance. As quickly as the pandemonium had begun, it subsided, the assailing Arabs either being shot or bayoneted. Wilson was still on his feet at the centre of the melee, broken sword in hand and his face smeared with the fresh blood from his scalp wound. The victory over the rebels was soon completed as Wilson returned back on board HMS *Hecla*. Word was already spreading of his gallantry and the decorations that would inevitably follow such an act of heroism in single combat.

The naval captain facing a savage enemy with his pith helmet sliced through to his scalp, still going forward with his broken sword in hand, was a story a patriotic Victorian back home received in awe, though Wilson was modest and surprised at the suggestion that he should be so honoured. He wrote:

> It has been a wonderful piece of luck as I only walked out on the morning as a loafer just to see the fight. The Admiral has, however, since put me down as accompanying him. Nothing was further from my thoughts than going for distinction of any kind.

Uppermost in his mind was to play down his feat and continue with his duty. As Winston Churchill was later to observe of Sir Arthur Knyvet Wilson, 'everything was duty. It was not merely that nothing else mattered. There was nothing else. One did one's duty as well as one possibly could, be it great or small and naturally one deserved no reward.'

Wilson's view was simpler:

> If I could only have got a basin of water and washed my face I should have escaped notoriety but I only had a little cold tea in my water bottle, and until we got to the wells, there was no water to be got, so the blood ran all over my face, and the correspondents spotted me.

Wilson was impressed by the courage and tenacity of his attackers regarding them as 'the most fearless creatures I have seen'.

*Sir Arthur Knyvet Wilson, VC.*

But there was high praise for Wilson's courage. The commander of the brigade at El Teb, Sir Redvers Buller, wrote of Wilson: 'It was one of the most courageous acts I have ever witnessed.'

When later Wilson arrived back in Britain, the *London Gazette* of 21st May 1884 carried confirmation of the award of the VC. It read:

> This Officer, on the staff of Rear-Admiral Sir William Hewett, at the Battle of El-Teb, on the 29th February 1884, attached himself during the advance to the right half battery, Naval Brigade, in the place of Lieutenant Royds, RN, mortally wounded.
>
> As the troops closed on the enemy's Krupp battery the Arabs charged out on the corner of the square and on the detachment who were dragging the Gardner

*The visitor to the beautiful Swaffham parish church will find much to admire. The memorial chapel on the south side contains the British Legion banners and various plaques, including that for Knyvet Wilson. The pictures on his plaque recognise that, as with Fisher, his time in the navy bridged the transition from sail to coal and oil.*

gun. Captain Wilson then sprang to the front and engaged in single combat with some of the enemy, thus protecting this detachment till some men of the York and Lancaster Regiment came to his assistance with their bayonets.

But for the action of this Officer, Sir Redvers Buller thinks that one or more of his detachment must have been speared. Captain Wilson was wounded but remained with the battery during the day.

Wilson was invested with his Victoria Cross by Commander-in-Chief Portsmouth, Admiral Sir George Phipps-Hornby, on Southsea Common, on 6th June 1884, in a ceremony watched by senior naval dignitaries and the entire crew of the *Hecla*. There were celebrations back in Swaffham for the local hero. Civic dignitaries poured praise on the modest Wilson.

Wilson's naval career flourished from that moment on. He had been at the *Vernon* torpedo school from 1876 but in 1888 returned to command *Vernon* until 1892 when he became ADC to Queen Victoria. Promoted rear admiral in 1895, he was given the role of carrying out secret torpedo-related manoeuvres from HMS *Hermione* before being called to the Admiralty in 1897 as Lord Commissioner of the Admiralty and Comptroller of the Navy. From 1901 to 1903 he was in command of the Channel Squadron and from 1903 he was Commander-in-Chief of the Home and Channel Fleets and widely admired and respected for the way he handled a large number of ships.

In *The Times* of Thursday, 26th May 1921 – in an assessment of his life under the heading 'A Great Admiral', the editorial said:

> During his long and brilliant period of supreme command Wilson achieved an unrivalled reputation alike as a fleet commander, a strategist and a tactician.

Knighted in 1902, Wilson was an influential figure in the development of the Royal Navy. His personality was austere; he was a man with an iron constitution and stoic endurance and known to his men as 'Old 'Ard 'Eart'. At times controversial, at others he was shy and modest. Although he performed a critical role in developing the torpedo as a weapon, he was not a great supporter of submarine warfare. He once famously described the submarine as 'a damned un-English weapon'.

In March 1907 he achieved the rank of admiral of the fleet, succeeding Lord Jacky Fisher of Kilverstone, and himself being succeeded in June 1908 by Tsar

Nicholas II of Russia, who held the post in an honorary capacity. He became First Sea Lord in 1910, similarly succeeding Fisher in that role. However, he accepted the position with a degree of reluctance and only after strong pressure was brought to bear on him by King Edward VII.

Wilson resigned early from his post as First Sea Lord in 1911 and retired from the Royal Navy in 1912. He was awarded the Order of Merit. Later, with Britain at war with Germany, Churchill invited him back to assist his successor, a role the Admiral accepted though only on the rather odd condition that he was not to be given an official post or salary.

Arthur Knyvet Wilson and Jacky Fisher were men of the same naval generation, of very similar ages, and the career of one followed the other, at times following a near-identical pattern: two great admirals and sea lords with Norfolk connections. But whereas Fisher often left conflict, controversy, feuding and division in his wake, Knyvet Wilson's style was more to calm the waters at the Admiralty.

Churchill described Wilson as 'the most selfless man I ever met or even read of. He wanted nothing, and he feared nothing – absolutely nothing.'

After the end of the war, Sir Arthur Knyvet Wilson did finally return to Swaffham and his home at Beech Cottage from where he enjoyed playing golf and dedicating time to help erect a memorial to the Norfolk town's war dead.

He received the title 3rd Baronet of Delhi in 1919, a title originally created for his uncle Sir Archdale Wilson in January 1858 for his command of the British troops in the Siege of Delhi in 1857 during the Indian Mutiny. The title became extinct on the death of Sir Arthur Knyvet Wilson at the age of 79 on 25th May 1921, some 37 years after the dramatic events at El Teb.

At his funeral, he was carried by four admirals and a vice admiral to burial in the churchyard of St Peter and St Paul, Swaffham. A memorial service was also held at Westminster Abbey. On 23rd April 1922, the bronze memorial plaque that remembers one of Norfolk's great sailors was unveiled in the church at Swaffham by Admiral Sir Edward Bradford. Wilson's Victoria Cross medal was donated to the Royal Naval Museum, Portsmouth.

# CHAPTER NINETEEN

# *John Loynes*

## (1843–1939)

John Loynes is regarded as the father of boating holidays on the Broads, a man whose idea and initiative created a tourism industry that now underpins and sustains numerous communities across swathes of Norfolk and Suffolk. Yet in the latter part of the 19th century, the Norfolk Broads was a quite different place to what it is today. The landscape was a wonderful wildlife habitat, but barely inhabited by the leisure sailing fraternity or holidaymakers.

The Broads evolved as a result of local people digging peat for heating and cooking purposes. The Romans and early Saxon settlers were among the first to discover the resource and took what they needed, but during the 9th to the 13th centuries peat extraction became more organised; the monks from St Benet's Abbey acquired the rights to it and became extremely wealthy in the process. Within the space of two centuries, nine million cubic feet (764,600m$^3$) of peat had been cut away, leaving deep, but evenly cut, holes in the landscape. However, during the 14th century the sea level rose, filling the chasms and flooding the area and forcing further peat digging to be abandoned.

The flooded, flat marshland became an important part of the landscape as the people who lived and worked there adapted to the changing terrain. The water became a transport artery, a means of communication, plied by trading vessels such as the famous Norfolk wherries for supplying villages with goods as well as carrying imports and exports to and from the coast. The Broads today boast 125 miles of navigable waterways and are a habitat for plants, animals, insects and birds.

During John Loynes' youth, the Broads were still commercial and were inhabited by the marshmen who worked on the land, maintaining the dykes and water levels, grazing cattle and making a living from the abundant resources of reed, hay, fish and wildfowl. Though beautiful, tranquil and unspoilt, the Broads were not then regarded as a potential tourist attraction. Loynes was to change all of that, though at first his idea was met with ridicule.

Born at Woodton near Brooke in 1843, John Loynes spent his early life as a village cobbler's boy and a brickyard worker. The 1851 census lists him as a boy of seven years old in the household of his 29-year-old father (also John), a journeyman shoemaker married to Hester, who was slightly older at 32 and was a straw bonnet maker. He had two brothers, Alfred and William, and a younger sister, Alice. A decade later, John Loynes had matured into a 16-year-old taking up appointment at Brooke Hall as a gentleman's servant in the employ of George Holmes who farmed 200 acres

*By the beginning of the 20th century the visitor to the Broads could hire a variety of vessels from a rowing boat to a pleasure wherry.*

nearby. In the grounds of the hall was a large lake, almost the size of Salhouse Broad, and on that the young Loynes learned to handle a small cutter-rigged boat. It was his first experience of sailing but one that was to have a profound impact on him and set the course for the rest of his long life.

On leaving Brooke Hall he went to Bungay where he used his savings to apprentice himself to a carpenter. He became proficient relatively quickly and soon left for London, living in the Shoreditch area, but the capital did not suit the rural boy who had developed a love of the waterways. Within a few years he moved back to Norwich, living on Elm Hill and working as a master craftsman.

Loynes spent much of his leisure time boating on the Wensum but found that the boats available to him in Norwich were too big to lift over the weirs and locks. Undeterred, and making use of his carpentry skills, he built a lighter boat suitable for that purpose. At the time – 1878 – he was living in Monastery Yard, Elm Hill and it was there that he built his first rowing boat, a vessel that was to become the forerunner of his Broads fleet. He would use a builder's handcart to take his boat to the Bure at Wroxham and from there explore the river and its Broads and the Thurne as far as Waxham Dyke. Loynes' outings in this boat saw him embark on mini voyages of exploration across the Broads before he eventually built a bigger and better boat, fully rigged with a cutter sail and capable of making the passage over Breydon. In later interviews, Loynes modestly conceded that his home-made vessel was an amateurish effort, but from this boat a leisure industry was to spring up. Loynes would occasionally take friends out in his boats for a trip often lasting a few days but he found that they kept stopping to inspect the fauna and flora. Eventually one of them asked, 'Why can't we hire the boat and please ourselves?'

Such chance remarks by friends and requests from tourists confirmed his suspicions that he was onto something: the building and letting of boats had the possibilities of a serious business project. Gradually, from the Elm Hill yacht station, a brisk hire business was to evolve and within a few years a whole new Norfolk industry.

Loynes would find holidaymakers and take them on waterborne tours. One of the most popular turned out to be an eight-day tour, departing from Monastery

*After Loynes had set the example, many others were soon on the advertising lists in the books that promoted the pleasures of a boating holiday on the Broads.*

| J. JIMPSON, WROXHAM. | Ten-ton Cabin and 3-ton Cabin Centre Board Una-Rig. Open, Sailing, and Rowing Boats, by the Day, Week, or Month, suitable for camping out on the Rivers and Broads. Yachting Parties supplied with every class of Provisions to order. |
|---|---|
| C. COOKE, WROXHAM. | STEAM LAUNCHES for Day Trips on Norfolk Broads, from Wroxham Station, G.E.R. |
| J. LOYNES, WROXHAM. | CABIN YACHTS from 23 tons to 3 Tons, fitted with every convenience for Cooking and Sleeping. Full particulars on application. Row Boats fitted with awnings, £2 to £1 10s. per week. |

THE BROAD DEMONS: enjoying(?) themselves.

*The success of Loynes' initiative and his imitators put a pressure onto the Broads which continues today.*

Staithe at Elm Hill at 3 o'clock in the morning. It was a tour that caught the eye of the public and the subsequent demand resulted in him in building larger boats for them to hire.

These vessels would sail away to Reedham, Breydon and Yarmouth and up the Bure to Acle, Horning and Wroxham and Coltishall. However, often at the end of a tour, the holidaymakers would leave the boat at Wroxham and Loynes had to return it to Norwich. He soon realised that Elm Hill was not a natural centre for the business so he moved the enterprise to Wroxham. Writing in the *Eastern Daily Press* on 24th August 1927, to mark Loynes' 84th birthday, the correspondent C. R. Chamberlin, noted that 'it was a very different Wroxham from that of today'. Chamberlin recalled that the young sailing entrepreneur's idea was laughed off by many.

> His project of setting up a boat hiring establishment met with ridicule. He had no money and no-one would finance him, but he believed in his quest and he stuck to it. His modus operandi was to secure a holidaymaker to sail him in the daytime to various points at which a bed and food could be obtained, and thus to traverse the Broads.

Loynes' designs evolved to meet the demand, first with canvas covers that could be used at night and then with his first cabin yacht. In time, and step by step, improvements came until his well known boats the *Victoria*, *Enterprise*, *Spree* and *Coral* formed 'an admirable fleet' and one that was to remain in the Loynes family until 1959.

> By this time, the news of Norfolk Broads yachting had spread, and others seeing the project they had ridiculed becoming a sound commercial proposition entered the arena, and Norfolk Broads yachting became an established form of holiday.

Chamberlin's account is confirmed in one of the early guides to the Broads by George Christopher Davies. The first edition of his *Handbook to the Rivers and Broads of Norfolk and Suffolk*, published in 1882, featured John Loynes as the only boat builder to advertise. Within ten years, there were 37 builders and owners listed as having boats for hire. At that time Davies noted: 'Each year the tourist stream increases, but, happily, there is still plenty of room.'

When he started in 1878, Loynes would charge £1 10s to £2 5s a week for a boat without an attendant, or four guineas with an attendant. Later he would run a fleet of yachts that ranged through 4, 6, 8, 10, 11, 14 and 17 tons and sleep from two to eight people. The weekly hire cost varied from £4 to £9 9s.

Writing in 1892 in *The Land of the Broads: A Practical and Illustrated Guide to the Broads of Norfolk and Suffolk*, Ernest Suffling made references to Loynes' fleet:

> Probably the largest fleet of yachts is owned by J. Loynes of Wroxham, who has had a number of years' experience of the requirements of amateur yachtsmen. He is, therefore, able to cater for them in a manner that other proprietors, not being used to the idiosyncrasies of the somewhat fastidious neophyte in cruising, cannot quite hit off so happily. His yachts embrace all sizes, from the queenly 17-tonner to the open 15 feet row boat, with its awning over for sleeping snugly beneath.
>
> The 17-ton yacht is very comfortable, and as it contains two cabins, has accommodation for ladies as well as gentlemen.

Suffling also tells us that a 'marked feature of Loynes' yachts and boats' is that they were all centreboard craft with a shallow draft that could go upon any of the Broads.

As Loynes' business grew, so did his family, which lived in the Hungate area of Norwich. According to the 1881 census, he and his wife Cecelia had seven children. At some point in the folowing decade Cecelia died, John Loynes married Mary Ann and they had another child.

In the 1890s, Loynes established an outpost of his hire business – Messrs John Loynes & Sons – in the Friesland Meres in Holland after hearing the terrain there was similar to the Broads, though ill-feeling towards the British on the outbreak of the South African War brought a premature end to this development on the other side of the North Sea. (The Boers who were fighting against the British were, of course, of Dutch origin.) However, Friesland remained a favourite holiday haunt of his for many years. Another outpost was established as far away as Canada, by his son Arnold in 1910.

Into his old age, John Loynes continued to develop holidaying on the Norfolk Broads and he would enthusiastically promote the destination, taking a 22-foot model of the terrain and his yachts to exhibitions in London and Birmingham. He also retained a passion for sailing, well into his old age. He paused for another interview with the *Eastern Daily Press* on the occasion of his 88th birthday, the correspondent describing him as 'active, alert, with a long-flowing beard'. He remained a traditionalist and despite the boats he had built in the interim he still preferred to sail in the simpler type of vessel he was building 50 years earlier.

John Loynes died on Sunday, 24th September 1939 after a short illness, less than a month after marking his 96th birthday. The great tradition of Broads boating holidays that John Loynes began in 1878 continues to this day. Still operating near the bridge at Wroxham, on the same site where Loynes first established his business in the town, is the company of Faircraft Loynes. Faircraft, set up in the late 1970s, merged with the Loynes company but to this day maintains the tradition the founder began of hiring boats out for tours and cruises on the Broads for holidaymakers.

*Loynes peers out from behind a canvas awning.*

# CHAPTER TWENTY

# Richard Woodget

## (1845–1928)

In the roll call of great British sailing ships, names such as the *Mary Rose*, *Golden Hind*, HMS *Victory* or *Warrior* spring readily to mind. There are also the *Titanic*, SS *Great Eastern* or even the *QE2* but few are more synonymous with speed, grace and beauty than the *Cutty Sark*.

During the famous sailing clipper's most successful period of service in the wool trade between Australia and the United Kingdom in the late 19th century, it was the son of a Norfolk farmer who took the helm to guide her with such agility between two great continents at opposite ends of the earth. So often, those crossings were in record time.

Richard Woodget became captain of the *Cutty Sark* in 1885. He had previously been master of the *Coldstream*, having learned his trade at sea as an apprentice on coasters off the east coast of Britain between Blyth and London after he left school. His command followed an unhappy period for the *Cutty Sark*, sparked by an unsavoury incident aboard on a voyage to the Far East in 1880. The mate, Sidney Smith, was provoked in a row by sailor John Francis and in the ensuing fight he beat the deckhand to death. The captain, James Wallace, had Smith arrested but then allowed him to escape. The crew were furious. They downed tools and stood on the verge of mutiny, leaving the vessel becalmed for three days in the Java Sea. For Wallace, it was the end of his career. Seeing little alternative for himself, he jumped overboard into waters that were infested with sharks. Lifeboats were lowered to try to rescue him, but Wallace had disappeared without trace.

Under the second mate, the ship limped back to Anjer, almost coming to grief on rocks near Thwart-the-Way island. Once at Singapore a new captain, called Bruce, was appointed but his tenure was short-lived. Regarded as incompetent following a crossing to New York, he was suspended and the entire crew paid off. The *Cutty Sark*, now in a state of disrepair and neglect, was a ship without a crew, or a cargo.

The owner, Captain Jock 'Old White Hat' Willis, solved the problem by transferring Captain F. W. Moore and his crew from the *Blackadder* to sail the *Cutty Sark* to London. Moore later took her on two voyages to Australia, proving just what she could do. With a crew at times pared down to 19 or 20, she sailed from the English Channel to Newcastle in New South Wales in 79 days and took 82 on the return leg, establishing the fastest passage of the year. Moore was promoted due to his success, which saw the *Cutty Sark* consistently outrun her old adversary *Thermopylae*. In turn, Woodget took over, an appointment that heralded the *Cutty Sark*'s 10-year dominance of the oceans.

The vessel he was to captain for the best part of the following decade had been launched at Dumbarton in 1869. She was sleek, beautiful and fast, the queen of the seas. Launched in the latter days of sail power, she was faster than the steamships that had been built to replace vessels of her ilk. Named after the short petticoat worn by the witch, Nannie, in the Robert Burns poem 'Tam O'Shanter', the *Cutty Sark* was 212 feet long, weighed 963 tons and with her 32,000 square feet of sail, she could reach 17 knots. In terms of power, she possessed the equivalent of a 3,000 horsepower engine.

Captain Willis was her first owner and his name is recorded in the bow with the motto: 'Where there's a Willis a way'.

Designed originally as a clipper for the tea run to China, she was first pitched against the *Thermopylae* in 1872. She was 400 miles ahead at one stage when disaster struck and the rudder broke. The *Cutty Sark* limped home, arriving a week after the rival vessel. The *Cutty Sark*'s career on tea runs to China was short-lived, with sailing clippers replaced by the steamships which were able to pass through the newly-opened Suez Canal. Her final tea run was in 1877.

By the time Woodget took over, with an annual salary of £186, the *Cutty Sark*'s days as a tea clipper were well behind her and she had a new role: transporting wool from Australia to Britain in time for the London wool sales. Under his captaincy, the clipper was to make several record-breaking passages between the UK and Australia. His apprenticeship on the coasters had served him well. He was a sailor who knew how to get the best out of a ship but he also had leadership qualities that set him apart from other skippers. His personal rule was that he would never let a crewman do anything he could not, or would not, do himself.

Woodget also often recruited his crew members from Norfolk.

Along with sailing, he had two other passions: breeding prize-winning sable collies – which were often found aboard the ship – and taking photographs. He took many pictures of the *Cutty Sark* in locations across the globe from Sydney Harbour to the Southern Ocean where the backdrop was often an iceberg. In one picture of the *Cutty Sark* at sail by Captain Woodget, the shot was taken in the open sea with a camera supported on a plank of wood fixed between two of the ship's boats.

On succeeding to the position of captain, Woodget was eager to see what his new ship could do on the wool route that would take her round Cape Horn and through the Roaring Forties. It soon transpired that Woodget and the *Cutty Sark* were made for one another. He left the East India Dock in London on 1st April 1885. The ship's log shows that he had crossed the equator just shy of three weeks later, was rounding the Cape on day 26 and arrived in Sydney on the 77th day of the voyage. The journey on the way back took 67 days from Sydney to the Channel, though calm conditions meant it took another five days to complete the final 300 miles. She still arrived home a week ahead of the *Thermopylae*.

In March 1887, the ship laden with wool, Woodget left Australia and made it back to London in 72 days. The following year, he cut the journey from New South Wales to Dungeness to 71 days against the 79 of the *Thermopylae*. On one glorious day, she made 363 nautical miles. In 1889, *Cutty Sark* was beaten by the *Nebo*, though both vessels arrived home in 82 days. But it was the last time she was pitched against the *Thermopylae*, which was sold to Canada to carry rice across the Pacific Ocean.

It was during this sailing, on the night of 25th July 1889, that the *Cutty Sark* was involved in a famous incident with the P&O steam ship *Britannia*. The steamer's second officer Robert Olivey observed the watch lights of a sailing ship overhauling his vessel, which itself was doing just under 16 knots. The *Britannia*'s crew did not know it was the *Cutty Sark* at the time but the steamship's log later noted: 'Sailing ship overhauled and passed us!'

In January 1893, after leaving Sydney for Antwerp, the *Cutty Sark* found itself in a large ice field and lost two men overboard. The following year, it transpired, was to be the last great race home from Australia for the famous vessel. She left Australia in December 1894 for Hull with more than 5,000 bales of wool aboard, arriving in the UK on 26th March 1895. But disembarkation brought dismay for Woodget, who discovered that Captain Willis had agreed to sell the *Cutty Sark* to a Portuguese firm, J. Ferreira & Co, for £2,100 and she became the *Ferreira* of Lisbon. The growing dominance of steamships in the wool trade runs, as the end of the 19th century neared, had left Willis with little alternative but to sell the *Cutty Sark*. Woodget was given *Coldinghame* to captain but was far from happy. After only one voyage aboard his new ship, he retired from the sea and bought a farm at Burnham Overy.

Woodget never lost his love of the sea and in retirement kept a small boat for sailing in the local creeks. He also sailed in regattas and taught younger people how to handle sail in all weathers. He remarried when he was 76 and farmed the land in north Norfolk until his death on 6th March 1928, aged 82. A carved stone anchor marks his final resting place in the churchyard of St Margaret's at Burnham Norton. For many years, Woodget was the local collector for the Shipwrecked Fishermen and Mariners Royal Benevolent Society and it was they who paid for the anchor.

However, life on the oceans was far from over for the *Cutty Sark*. She worked for the next 26 years and by 1922 was the only working clipper ship left in the world.

In January 1922, the fortunes of the *Cutty Sark* – or *Ferreira* – had changed again. She sought refuge in Falmouth during a storm and was spotted there by Captain Wilfred Dowman, who had always admired her since passing close by in 1894 while on the *Hawksdale* during his apprenticeship. After negotiating a price with the Portuguese owners, he bought the *Cutty Sark* and a process of restoration began. Two years later, there was one final nostalgic journey for Woodget. Following the restoration, he was persuaded out of retirement to take over nominal command for a few days in 1924 – almost three decades after last leaving the ship – to sail on her to Fowey. It was the final chapter in the *Cutty Sark* story for the Woodget family.

*Captain Richard Woodget, master of the* Cutty Sark.

Captain Woodget was born at Burnham Norton on 21st November 1845 and had four sons. Richard jnr, Harold and Sydney were all indentured to their father and served on the *Cutty Sark*, while Edgar decided against going to sea.

Richard Woodget jnr served four years' apprenticeship under his father and a year as second mate and one as mate. He was a captain with the Blue Funnel Line sailing out of Liverpool and at one time commanded the *Anchises*. He also served on HMS *King George V* from 1944 until the end of World War 2, having previously been on HMS *Revenge* and HMS *Iron Duke* when she was bombed in Scapa Flow. He also recalled seeing the sinking of HMS *Royal Oak* when he was a gunner. Later awarded the MBE, he retired to Burnham Overy Staithe. Harold served with the British Steamship Company while Sydney commanded a ship that plied the route between Europe and China.

Captain Richard John Woodget jnr was the eldest and last surviving of the brothers. He died at King's Lynn in 1965 aged 93. But six years earlier, in an interview with the *Eastern Daily Press*, he recalled life aboard the *Cutty Sark* under his father, reflecting on the austere conditions, meals of salt beef and biscuit and perils of life high up the mast as the vessel rounded the Cape. He never forgot the thrill of 'sailing round the world being blown by trade winds and squalls' and of how nothing could 'quell his father's desire for speed'.

As a permanent reminder of those days, he kept a five-foot scale model of the *Cutty Sark* in his room. It had been made by an Australian and was given to him in Sydney in 1929. Woodget jnr recalled his father being a 'damned hard commander' with the journeys to Australia leaving an impact on the crew members. 'One voyage was enough for most of them,' he recalled in 1959. 'A lot of them came from King's Lynn, and the families there have plenty to say about what an old tartar he was.'

Two years after the *Cutty Sark*'s last commercial owner Captain Dowman died in 1936, his widow presented the clipper to the Thames Nautical Training College so that she could be used to train both Royal Navy and Merchant Navy officers. Later refurbished in Blackwall in 1951, she was moored above Greenwich to be admired by visitors to the Festival of Britain. She was fully overhauled in 1954 before being moved to her final resting place in the purpose-built dry dock at Greenwich. Her official opening by the Queen in 1957 was considered of such significance that the occasion was broadcast live by the BBC.

On the morning of 21st May 2007, the nation awoke to television images of one of the country's best-loved vessels ablaze at its London moorings. The ferocity of the flames was shocking to see, but many fixtures, fittings and half the original timbers had been removed as part of an ambitious £25m refurbishment, which meant the damage was less severe than initially appeared. Three decks were still seriously damaged, but the project to restore the *Cutty Sark* to her former glory resumed. It was a close call, but the ship Woodget guided so swiftly between England and Australia survived and will continue to be a treasured part of the nation's maritime heritage.

*Woodget's grave with its memorial anchor lies in the churchyard at Burnham Norton. The text appropriately reads, 'So he bringeth them unto their desired haven.'*

# CHAPTER TWENTY-ONE

# Reverend Ebenezer Mather

## (1849–1927)

Around the coastline of the United Kingdom a welfare organisation cares for the maritime community and their families. Known as the Royal National Mission to Deep Sea Fishermen (RNMDSF), it distributes aid, welfare, advice and support as well as spiritual assistance and guidance to the fishing community.

While it has for many years had a national presence, its origins lie in Norfolk where, at the time of its foundation, the harbours were the heart of the world's herring fishing industry. The RNMDSF can trace its beginnings directly to the concerns voiced for the wellbeing of the maritime community by a priest serving in the county.

When the reports of the perilous conditions that fishermen were forced to endure, as they landed their catch in the latter part of the 19th century, reached Ebenezer Mather, he was surprised and even shocked. The men of the smacks worked in arduous conditions with little emotional, physical or spiritual support. The casualty rate was high and medical provision was virtually non-existent. In addition, the fishermen were at the mercy of the 'copers'. These foreign grog ships, selling alcohol out on the ocean waves, preyed on the men of the British shipping fleets.

Mather felt the need for an organisation that not only supported these men at sea but also offered the fishermen and their families care in their own communities, particularly at times of tragedy. He already had a reputation as a man of action, not just words, within the church community and decided to board one of the vessels to see for himself exactly what life at sea was like in those dark days. He went to experience the conditions, to talk to the fishermen and discover at first hand the limited support and help that was available to them in times of trouble. He also took with him the word of God, determined to offer these fishermen the spiritual guidance he felt would give them added strength and endurance in their work.

In 1881, Ebenezer Mather boarded a smack and sailed out to visit the fishing fleet on the Dogger Bank. It was a perilous journey for a land-based priest and clearly an eye-opening experience for the Norfolk clergyman. From it, he produced his book *"Nor'ard of the Dogger"* which gives a vivid account of his time aboard.

> Fish appeared on my table, for aught I knew it might have grown on the Fishmonger's slab! Let those who speak of the price of fish spend one night aboard a trawling smack. You must be prepared for the grey wilderness of a floating ocean, swept by winds as cold and pitiless as the hand of death!

Mather was appalled by the degrading conditions in which fishermen worked and lived. His response was swift and led him to found the National Mission to Deep Sea Fishermen to alleviate their plight.

After that first trip on the smack, Mather said in his account:

> I saw sin shorn of its attractions and revealed in all its naked hideousness. Not only the degrading damning drink traffic but other forms of sin only to be mentioned with bated breath, and for which the Divine writings reserve the most scathing rebuke.

He came back to Gorleston and raised £1,000 to buy the first 'bethel' or chapel ship to be manned by Christian fishermen and sail with the fleets offering the support, comfort and medical care the men needed.

In 1882, the *Ensign* was ready and sailed from Great Yarmouth, which was still a major and important fishing port. It carried warm clothes, tobacco, medical equipment and Bibles. With her 20-foot Mission flag flying in the breeze as she left under Captain Budd, the *Ensign* was jeered, as well as cheered, by those on the harbour side. There were those who felt it was the waste of a good fishing vessel. Unperturbed, its crew headed to where the smacks operated and during the week fished alongside them. On a Sunday, it became a Mission ship, with smacksmen crowding aboard to buy their supplies of tobacco. The vessel had a small library but, more significantly, a medical chest. Medical treatment was badly needed out

*The* Ensign *leaves Great Yarmouth for the first time, in an engraving from Mather's own book* "Nor'ard of the Dogger". *The engraving is from a drawing by J. R. Wells and C. J. Staniland, who recorded many east coast scenes before photography completely took over.*

at sea and it was not unknown for an injured man to remain at sea for up to three months before getting ashore to receive proper attention.

Mather was convinced that the worst enemy of the men aboard the smacks were the Dutch copers, or grog ships. They would sell a bottle of gin for a shilling, rum for 1s 6d and brandy for two shillings. These vessels preyed on the crews, but Mather was determined to offer them an alternative to cheap alcohol. The men who worked aboard these vessels, in the most treacherous conditions, were among the more vulnerable in society.

Writing in his account of life aboard the fishing vessels of the North Sea in *North Sea Fishers and Fighters* (1911), Walter Wood said life at sea was 'rough and hard, and mostly cruel'.

The savage discipline of the old Navy, when the lash was used to flog men into obedience, was reflected in the North Sea smacks, and the unhappy little fellows who were sent to the fleets from the workhouse, or packed off by a magistrate in preference to sending them to gaol, were entirely at the

*The Mission smack* Sir William Archibald.

mercy of men some of whom did not show mercy or kindness because they had never known it in their own lives of brutal sordid toil.

The departure of the *Ensign* was a start, and from that moment, Ebenezer Mather became the original 'fishermen's friend'.

Later Mission ships – some of them steamers – had a sick bay and cots for the injured; at times there was also a surgeon on board. By 1886, the *Euston* sailed from Yarmouth as the third bethel ship and a year later the first hospital mission

*Above: the Mission smack* Alice Fisher. *Below: the Mission steamer* Queen Alexandra.

ship was launched. In 1896, Queen Victoria granted the Mission the title 'Royal', which it still proudly uses today.

The Mission fleet expanded with vessels carrying such names as *Sir William Archibald*, *Queen Alexandra*, *Sir Edward P. Willis* or *Alice Fisher*. Some were specifically built for the mission, notably *Sophia Wheatley*, which was launched out of Yarmouth in 1887. She had the outward appearance of an ordinary smack but below decks she had some specific modifications. These included cabins for missionaries and lockers for several tons of 'cut Cavendish' tobacco. The work of the Mission ships is vividly illustrated in an extract from the skipper's log at the time:

> Feb. 13, 1888. 7 came for medical aid and one poor man came this morning with 2 of his ribs broken. Bound him up and then spoke to him of a loving Saviour.

Despite the growing fleet, which was proving such a success with the Mission work, Mather was already looking beyond the conditions aboard the fishing smacks, examining the needs of the men once they returned to shore and the conditions the fishermen's families endured on land. To him, around this time, it became apparent that care and support for fishermen was needed in ports as well as offshore.

The RNMDSF embarked on a project to build hostels and institutes with canteens. The first was in Gorleston High Street. A plaque marking the 125th anniversary of the founding of the Mission was unveiled in 2006 on the site of the original Gorleston office, though the base in this region has since relocated to Lowestoft.

By the end of the 19th century the Mission had spread as far as Newfoundland with medical boats tending to fishermen there. During the war years the Mission looked after crews of sunken ships and many of its vessels were drafted into service sweeping the seas for mines.

Those who need help do not need to belong to the Mission, or share the faith. All that is asked is that they belong to the fishing community. Today, the Mission has a presence in over 70 ports and harbours with 17 superintendents covering the busiest ports. In a typical year, 3,000 fishermen and their families receive financial support, 170,000 meals are served to members of fishing communities, 12,000 home visits are made and 240 shipwrecked or injured fishermen are given emergency assistance.

The Mission has also responded to the changing face of the fishing industry. There are fewer ships operating from fewer ports but the work of the RNMDSF continues as Mather would have envisaged, caring for the families and the men of the trawlers. Since the early 1950s, the Mission has been a shore-based organisation. Nowadays, it concentrates on providing land-based welfare to sick, disabled, distressed and retired fishermen and their families.

While the Mission has changed and adapted to meet the needs and demands of a fishing community since, its work still remains crucial in the welfare of the fishing families. There is still a strong presence in the east at Lowestoft docks with its work continuing, most recently under the eye of a port missioner covering Essex, Suffolk and Norfolk offering Christian welfare and support to the fishing community.

It is a far cry from the days, even in the 1960s, when it was possible to walk from north Lowestoft to south Lowestoft stepping from one boat to another. Lowestoft was one of the five major fishing ports in the country, but now there are only nine or ten longshore fishing boats. But the retired fishermen, their widows and their children remain and are cared for. Even now, the Lowestoft office has a caseload of about 300 people.

The Mission has a head office in Hampshire and is funded by public donation; there is no state aid or grants. But it has adapted with the times and those who still serve it remain convinced that its founder would be just as pleased with the mission as it is now.

*The Fishermen's Welfare Centre at Lowestoft today, by the entrance to the fish dock.*

Ebenezer Mather died in 1927. He is buried in the graveyard of St Katherine's Church, Canvey Island in Essex. His gravestone reads: 'In affectionate remembrance of The Fishermen's Friend Ebenezer Joseph Mather, founder of the Royal National Mission for Deep Sea Fishermen called home on December 23rd, 1927 aged 78 years.'

*Ebenezer Mather, saviour of souls through the founding of the Royal National Mission to Deep Sea Fishermen.*

# CHAPTER TWENTY-TWO

# *Thomas Crisp*

## (1876–1917)

As a boy, the sea had a magical lure for Thomas Crisp. The Swedish and Russian schooners moored in Lowestoft harbour with their intriguing cargoes fascinated him, so much so that he often spent more time on the quayside than behind his desk in the classroom at nearby St John's National School.

Eventually, concerned at the distraction these foreign vessels moored so close to school were having on his son, his father William Crisp moved Thomas to the British School in London Road to finish his education.

Thomas Crisp was born on 28th April 1876, one of at least nine children but after leaving school he showed little inclination to follow in his father's footsteps as a shipwright, instead preferring to man the vessels that had attracted him as a young boy. He spent some time on the smacks fishing for herring and mackerel and then sought further adventure as a crewman aboard an ocean-going liner between London and New York.

As the clouds of war darkened over Europe, he joined the Royal Naval Reserve, initially as a deckhand. Soon after, he gained his commission and went as skipper of one the armed decoy smacks, which at the time were the Royal Navy's 'secret weapon' to be pitted against the German U-boats that roamed the North Sea. The enemy vessels had enjoyed almost free range of the sea lanes, virtually picking off British shipping at will until the introduction of the armed smacks that were known as 'Q' ships. They were remarkably successful, accounting for the loss of up to 14 German submarines.

In the earlier part of the war, German U-boat commanders had been in the habit of surfacing close to fishing smacks, ordering the crew off and allowing the men to escape in a small boat then sinking the vessel. After a while, the navy became aware of an opportunity for counter-attack and began fitting some of these smacks with a small gun capable of inflicting severe damage or even sinking these submarines. To the unobserved – and the unwary eye – they were no more than fishing smacks, plying a legitimate trade in the waters of the North Sea. They caught and landed their catch regularly at ports such as Lowestoft.

But these small, highly-manoeuvrable vessels now also had this other, secret,

*Tom Crisp and his family.*

role. Taken over by the Admiralty, they were manned with Royal Navy and Royal Naval Reserve personnel, fitted with engines and the discreet single, yet potentially deadly, gun. The technique was simple: when the submarine surfaced, the smack's crew lined up on deck in front of the gun and then ducked out of the way at the last moment as a highly-accurate shell was unleashed. On a number of occasions the U-boat was mortally wounded, often sinking before it could respond.

By 1st February 1917, Thomas Crisp was an accomplished 'Q' ship skipper. His son, Thomas William Crisp, had a couple of years earlier lied about his age and joined the Navy as a 16-year-old. By winter 1917, having made the right contacts, he had arranged to be transferred to Lowestoft to serve on a 'Q' ship as mate under his father on the smack *I'll Try*.

On that cold morning of the first day of February, the *I'll Try* had encountered a submarine and was forced into playing a potentially deadly game of seaborne cat and mouse with it as the German U-boat sought out the English vessel. With their engines, the smacks were swift and agile and could often outwit the lumbering U-boats.

Suddenly, the submarine came at the *I'll Try*, only yards away. In an instant the smack opened fire with its 13–pounder, hit the sub full on between the conning tower and the deck and sent it down to the depths, head first, crippled and

*Right:* LT649, *then known as the* G and E, *and a crew before World War 1. She would later be known as the* I'll Try *and then as* Nelson *when under the command of Tom Crisp.*

*Below:* LT649, *still in her time as the* G and E, *passes between the piers of Lowestoft harbour, as she would later in her wartime service.*

sinking. For his gallantry in this action Thomas was awarded the Distinguished Service Cross, which he later received from King George V, along with £200.

Recognising his ability, the Royal Navy offered him a position on board a special service ship. But as his 39-year-old wife Harriet (the mother of his three children, Thomas William, Harriet May and Charles Montgomery) was dying he chose to remain skipper of the smack and closer to home.

By the summer of 1917 the atmosphere had changed among the fishing fraternity. Any sense of chivalry and 'fair play' by German commanders had evaporated and the smacks, armed or unarmed, were considered fair game. U-boat commanders now surfaced more warily after they had suffered at the hands of these seemingly innocuous British fishing smacks.

In August 1917, the *I'll Try* had been renamed *Nelson*, a policy designed to retain the secret status of the Q ship. On the afternoon of Wednesday 15th, the *Nelson* – skippered by Thomas who was by now a widower – was in the vicinity of Jim Howe Bank off Lowestoft with the smack *Ethel and Millie* close by.

At around 2.45 p.m., the crews noticed an enemy submarine approaching fast. Skipper Crisp called for his glasses for a closer look and immediately sang out: 'Clear for action. Submarine.'

The German vessel started firing and with its fourth shot hit the *Nelson* just below the water line. The smack returned fire but the submarine lay just out of reach of her guns. A description of what happened next is best left to Thomas Crisp junior, who recalled the events of that tragic afternoon in his memoirs, written in 1958.

This went on for awhile, until one shell hit my father on the right hip and blew both legs and the lower part of his body away. But he kept conscious, how I don't know and told us to send a message off by pigeon saying 'send help, *Nelson* being attacked by submarine, skipper killed,' and then told us to throw the confidential books overboard and then he asked to be thrown overboard himself.

All this was happening when shells were bursting around us all the time but me taking the place of my father at the tiller, we continued to fire until our ship was nearly awash. I then gave orders for the small boat to be got out and abandon ship.

The crew soon did this and got into the boat, leaving me and my poor father on the smack alone. I knelt down beside him and kissed him goodbye, he did not speak or make any sign that he knew what was happening, so I think my father had passed away.

*A visit to the Lowestoft Maritime Museum will give the background to the service carried out by east coast fishermen on drifters and trawlers during both world wars. Tom Crisp junior, serving on board with his father when he was killed, was an honoured member of the society which helped establish the museum.*

Thomas jnr then leapt over the stern into the small boat and turned to see the *Nelson* going down, taking the remains of his father with her. His body was never recovered.

The submarine later turned its guns on the *Ethel and Millie* as its crew abandoned ship.

> The last we saw of the *Ethel and Millie*'s crew was standing on the foredeck of the sub with their hands above their head. They were never heard of again.

The surviving crew of the *Nelson* still were not safe and feared the U-boat commander would come after them. Miraculously, a fog came down, shrouding the handful of men in a small boat. Thomas jnr, still only 18, took charge. Instead of heading for land, as the submarine might have expected, the men chose to row out to sea. Some 48 hours later, they came across the Jim Howe Shoal buoy 40 miles out to sea and clung to it, before being picked up by the gunboat *Dryad*.

Within weeks, a Victoria Cross 'trial' was held, examining the conduct of

*Tom Crisp, VC, wearing his DSC.*

Skipper Thomas Crisp and his crew. On 15th October 1917, it was announced he would be awarded the VC. Thomas jnr later received his 41-year-old father's posthumous VC from King George V and his own Distinguished Service Medal for his actions on that day. The *Nelson*'s gunlayer, Leading Seaman Percival Ross, was awarded a bar to his DSM. The courageous deeds of the 'Q' ships and their crews became a little less secret when on 29th October 1917 the Prime Minister, David Lloyd George, gave an account of their heroics to Parliament.

After the war, and up until World War 2, Thomas Crisp senior was often referred to as the hero Skipper Crisp. His son Thomas jnr continued as a fisherman before later joining the crews on the Lowestoft and Ness Point tugs, ending his working life as bridge-keeper in the town. He died in 1979.

On the 50th anniversary of the action, he donated his father's VC to Lowestoft so that the people of the town could see it. For many years, a picture of Skipper Crisp hung in the council chamber close to the medal. The base metal medal is particularly rare in that the ribbon of Crisp's VC is blue, for a naval hero, as opposed to the regular deep maroon. That colouring makes it exceptionally valuable and now the original is kept in the vaults of the Waveney District Council offices. Replicas have been made and are on show to visitors who request to see them.

Skipper Crisp was just an ordinary fisherman from Burgh St Peter and Lowestoft who displayed the most incredible bravery. With his dying words 'Tom, I'm done for, throw me overboard,' his name is forever recalled in local folklore.

The story of Thomas Crisp's heroics, dying from appalling injuries sustained in a one-sided duel with a German U-boat yet still commanding the smack until it sank beneath him, is one of the most courageous of World War 1. As a seaman from a seagoing community, Crisp served his country in the way he knew best and selflessly made the ultimate wartime sacrifice to defend British shores.

# CHAPTER TWENTY-THREE

# *Henry Blogg*
## (1876–1954)

In the first half of the 20th century, hundreds of souls could count on their lives thanks to Henry Blogg and the lifeboat crews he led, without fear, into the treacherous conditions in the North Sea off the Norfolk coast. In peacetime and during two world wars, Blogg risked his own life on numerous occasions to save those in peril on the deep. A legend in his own lifetime, Coxswain Blogg remains the most decorated lifeboat man ever and at the height of his career, despite his personal modesty, was a personality as well known as the leading sporting and film stars of the day.

Born in a cottage in New Street, Cromer, on 6th February 1876, Henry George Blogg lived all his life in the town, fashioning a living through a beach hut and deckchair hire business and also as a crab fisherman. That was the job he took after leaving school when he was barely 12 and it was during this time that he witnessed the incident that helped shape his thoughts of joining the lifeboat crews.

The son of Ellen Blogg, he was raised by the family of James Davies who was a coxswain of the Cromer lifeboat. In 1888, young Henry saw the rescue of passengers from the steamer *Victoria*, which was in trouble. Six years later, at the age of 18, Blogg first joined the Cromer lifeboat. He served for eight years as a member of the crew of the rowing lifeboat *Benjamin Bond Cabbell*, the following seven years as second coxswain, and in 1909 he became coxswain.

It was on the bleak night of 9th January 1917, that Henry Blogg truly came of age as a lifeboat man. The Swedish steamer SS *Fernebo* had run aground off

Cromer after hitting a mine. The explosion had ripped her in two with both parts drifting in stormy conditions towards the beach. What followed was a rescue that the RNLI Heritage Trust describes as 'one of the most courageous and spectacular services ever undertaken by lifeboat men around our shores'.

For Blogg and the crew, whose average age was over 50, it was the second launch of the day as they had already been to the aid of the *Pyrin*. After several abortive launch attempts, they rowed in an open boat to the wreck, 400 yards off shore. It was still in the days when many lifeboats relied on little more than the grit, determination and the brute strength of those who manned it to row out to ships in trouble. By the time they were alongside the stricken *Fernebo*, they had been out in the elements for almost 14 hours.

The mission was a success, with all 11 crew members from half of the *Fernebo* taken safely ashore. Every man aboard the lifeboat *Louisa Heartwell* on that day was decorated and Blogg won the first of his three RNLI Gold Medals, regarded as the 'lifeboat VC'.

In 1924, Blogg was awarded the Empire Gallantry Medal by King George V. When in 1940 King George VI introduced the George Cross as the highest

*The young Henry Blogg is second from the left in the back row of this photograph of the crew of the* Louisa Heartwell *lifeboat. At that time Jimmy 'Buttons' Harrison was coxswain; he handed over to Blogg in 1909.*

civilian honour for bravery and to rank alongside the Victoria Cross, recipients could exchange their gallantry medals for the George Cross, which Blogg accepted in 1941.

A decade after the heroics of the *Fernebo* incident, Blogg was involved in the rescue of 15 men from the Dutch tanker *Georgia* in November 1927. It had split into two with crew members trapped on both sections, which were drifting. The steamer *Trent* rescued the men in the stern while the crew of the lifeboat *H. F. Bailey* managed to save the men in the bow, who were trapped in the bridge with the vessel stuck on a sandbank. For this rescue Blogg received his second Gold Medal and a gold watch from the Queen of Holland. Cromer bells pealed and crowds cheered after the crew arrived ashore following the rescue. In 1932, he played a leading role in the rescue of the crew from the 5,000-tonne Italian steamer *Monte Nevoso*, which had broken its back on Haisbro Sands. He rescued 30 men and a dog, the latter rescue winning him a Silver Medal from the Canine Defence League. Another dramatic rescue was of the 65-ton barge *Sepoy* on 13th December 1933, where Blogg drove the lifeboat onto the deck of the stricken vessel and held it firm long enough for the crew to leap aboard. Between these high-profile rescues, there were many other life-saving launches with Blogg as coxswain.

Blogg, a father of two, gained his third 'lifeboat VC' in August 1941 when he and his crews saved 88 lives from a convoy of six British ships aground on Haisbro Sands. When the lifeboats arrived, several of the vessels were already starting to break up with some 119 crew still stranded aboard. Two lifeboats from Cromer and those from Yarmouth, Gorleston, Sheringham and Lowestoft were involved. But it was Cromer number one boat, with Blogg at the wheel, that played the lead role.

When Blogg's boat arrived at the scene just before 10 a.m., the first steamer had only two masts, a funnel and upper works above the water with no obvious sign of life aboard. But as he headed for the second vessel, the crew spotted men hanging from behind the funnel of the first ship. Blogg steered his lifeboat back towards them, driving it over the submerged deck and repeatedly into a crack in her bow until 16 men were hauled board. A further 31 men were rescued from the second ship by Blogg's crew and transferred to a destroyer before the lifeboat returned to collect 19 men from a third vessel, again by driving the lifeboat over the steamer's bulwarks and submerged deck and holding her against the bridge while the men leapt to safety.

During World War 2, Cromer lifeboat station's record was the best in the country and from 1939 to 1945 the two motor lifeboats were launched 155 times

*Henry Blogg was well beyond the age when a lifeboat coxswain would normally retire when he reached the peak of his fame during World War 2. This portrait was taken by Sheringham photographer Olive Edis.*

and saved 450 lives. Perhaps the most demanding rescue undertaken by Blogg was when the *English Trader* ran aground off Cromer in October 1941. Blogg was 65 when his lifeboat *H. F. Bailey* put out in a full gale blowing from the north-north-east. The *H. F. Bailey* was the most famous lifeboat he served on and had the operational number of 777 – lucky seven, trebled. The boat was based at Cromer from 1935 to 1945 – throughout World War 2 – and was launched 120 times during this period saving 520 lives. The vessel can still be seen in the Henry Blogg Museum in Cromer.

When Blogg reached the *English Trader*, the conditions were appalling with seas running from both directions along the hull, some of the waves reaching mast height. Five men had been washed overboard, though 44 were still on the ship. At the second attempt to move in, at about 1 p.m., the lifeboat was overwhelmed by a mass of water; and several members of the crew, including Blogg, were washed overboard. Blogg was unable to swim, but another crew member threw him an aircraft dinghy which he clung to and was hauled back aboard. With signalman Walter Allen dying from heart failure Blogg turned the lifeboat for Yarmouth harbour, but at first light the next morning the lifeboat headed again for the *English Trader*. After a night of despair, all 44 men finally climbed aboard Cromer lifeboat and were taken to safety.

What set Blogg apart was that he was the type of leader that made other brave men 'even braver'. He was trusted by those around him and respected for his skill and personal courage. But above that, he knew what his boat could do and he knew what the sea could do. Despite this, he still took risks, because he felt that was his duty as a lifeboat man. Blogg was modest with his courage, rarely seeking to highlight his exploits, and would ask what 'all the fuss was about' when much was made of a particular rescue.

A former Chief Inspector of lifeboats, Commander T. G. Michelmore, said:

> That was Henry Blogg, a man who belittled his own gallant actions and a man who disliked intensely any form of publicity, in which he would take no part unless he could be assured that in doing so he would further the interests of the RNLI to whose ideals he was intensely loyal.

In the later years of his career, Blogg continued to be honoured, even after his retirement in 1947. His retirement gifts, presented later, included an illuminated inscription, which read:

> In the 72 years that you have lived in Cromer, and particularly during the 53 years that you have served the RNLI, you have, by your deeds and example, brought great credit upon the town, which is proud to call you citizen, and upon the lifeboat service.

In August 1948, Cromer's number one lifeboat was named after him by Admiral of the Fleet Sir John Cunningham, the vessel then under the command of his nephew Coxswain Henry 'Shrimp' Davies (1914–2002). A portrait of Coxswain Blogg by T. C. Dugdale appeared on a set of nine postage stamps in 1950, with others including lifeboat heroine Grace Darling and lifeboat service founder Sir William Hillary.

Blogg died in Cromer Hospital on 13th June 1954 aged 78. Four days later, up to 3,000 people attended his funeral service at the Church of St Peter and St Paul in Cromer. About 1,400 packed the parish church while many more waited outside in the churchyard to hear the service. In the days before the funeral, hundreds had filed past his coffin in the chancel of the church. At the service, on the afternoon of 17th June 1954, former Home Secretary and Foreign Secretary Lord Templewood, who was president of the Cromer branch of the RNLI at the time, talked of Blogg's courage.

> We knew him to be one of the bravest men who ever lived. I am told that some of his rescues were so courageous that they would have been thought rash and foolhardy if it had not been for the skill with which he saved the situation. Regardless of the sea and the dangers ahead, he would drive the lifeboat on to the wreck as he drove it when he saved the convoys off Haisbro Sands in 1941.
> So fine a leader of men, inspired the fullest confidence in the crew. They

would follow him anywhere, for they knew that he had both the courage to face the danger and the skill to surmount it.

. . . A very gallant man of simple tastes, great courage and strong character. His exploits are known to the whole nation.

Flags in the town flew at half mast and as the coffin was brought from the church, two lifeboat maroons – similar to those which so many times had called Henry Blogg and his crew into the dangers of the North Sea – were fired in salute. His decorations were carried by the bowman of the Cromer lifeboat Mr Kelly Harrison while four Norfolk coxswains bore the coffin. A lorry laden with 100 wreaths followed. A year after his death, a memorial fund had raised money to build a shelter in a garden in his memory. There is also a memorial bust on the cliff top in Cromer with him looking out to sea.

Henry Blogg's career as a lifeboat man is unsurpassed in the history of off-shore rescue in this country. It was his frequent and consistent acts of gallantry that played a key part in saving hundreds of lives off the Norfolk coastline. The RNLI note: 'His impact on the RNLI was immense and his exploits off the coast of Norfolk did more than anything else to endear the RNLI to the British public in the first half of the 20th century.'

During his 53 years of service, 38 of them spent as coxswain, the lifeboats went out on 387 occasions. They saved 873 lives.

*Left: Henry Blogg's gold medal with its two bars. His full set of medals is on display at the Henry Blogg Lifeboat Museum on the east promenade at Cromer (pictured below).*

CHAPTER TWENTY-FOUR

# *William Fleming*

## (1865–1954)

William Fleming was older than his counterpart in north Norfolk, Henry Blogg, but despite the dangers of their roles as lifeboat men, the two coxswains survived into grand old age. By coincidence, both died in 1954.

William George Fleming was born in Gorleston in 1865 and spent his early life working small vessels under sail on the east coast. The Census of 1881 shows Fleming as a 16-year-old ordinary seaman serving on the *Charlotte Cole* in a crew that consisted of master, mate, three able seamen, three ordinary seamen and one boy seaman.

Coxswain 'Billy' Fleming lived for most of his life in Pavilion Road, Gorleston, a short sprint from the lifeboat shed. That gave him time to haul on his heavy leather boots and gabardine coat and dash to the boat as the maroons summoned him and other crew members for another rescue.

When he joined the lifeboat crews in the mid 1880s, Fleming would have been acutely aware of the dangers he was exposing himself to. In 1881, six lifeboat men from the Great Yarmouth boat the *Abraham Thomas* had drowned when their vessel overturned in heavy seas while attempting to rescue a seaman from the stranded schooner *Guiding Star* and in 1888 four crew from the private Gorleston lifeboat *Refuge* drowned while heading to the aid of a steamer.

Through the later years of the 19th century and spanning the first four decades of the 20th century, Fleming served aboard the Gorleston lifeboats and as coxswain from 1922 to 1934. Over his 49-year career he helped rescue 1,188 people and was decorated with the Empire Gallantry Medal (which like Blogg he later

*Coxswain Fleming did his duty for publicity for the RNLI in a photographer's studio, but perhaps felt less than comfortable in this environment.*

exchanged for the George Cross), the RNLI's Gold Medal, a Silver Medal and three Bronze Medals.

Fleming was in his late 50s, a ruddy-cheeked and moustachioed fisherman, when he took over as coxswain in 1922. Soon after that he was to become involved in his most famous and treacherous rescue, an ordeal of courage and determination that would stretch into two exhaustive days at sea in the most foul of conditions.

The South Shields-based collier *Hopelyn* had left her home port bound for London on 18th October 1922, laden with 3,400 tons of coal. As she steamed off the east coast, the steering gear broke in a north-easterly gale. With a crew of 24 aboard, along with their mascot of a black cat named Tishy, she decided to try to seek shelter in Yarmouth Roads. But as makeshift repairs to the steering gear again failed, in worsening conditions, any hope of finding shelter deteriorated. The ship dropped anchors but they had little effect against the ferocity of the storm. The ship's officer recorded: 'There was nothing for it but to drift, and it was no surprise when we got on the north of Scroby Sands.'

*Hopelyn* sent out an SOS just in time: moments later, a wave swept away the wireless mast. It was almost 9.30 p.m. and the vessel began to break up. The crew initially sheltered beneath the bridge but then all 24 of them were forced to seek refuge in the highest part of the ship, the 12-foot square wireless room. With her back broken, the *Hopelyn* was beyond salvation. The crew, and the terrified cat, were trapped in the tiny radio shack as the mountainous waves pounded away at a ship that was slowly disintegrating beneath them.

seas were washing over the poor fellows. They waved their arms, and above the noise of the storm could be heard murmurs of thanksgiving.

Swan skilfully manoeuvred his vessel alongside, holding position for as long as possible as the crew of the *Hopelyn* left their tiny refuge and scrambled down ropes aboard the motor lifeboat in fours, along with their cat. The rescue had taken more than 30 hours in total but by that morning of 21st October 1922, every man – and animal – was safe.

Coxswain Fleming was awarded a Gold Medal, with 15 Bronze Medals awarded to the crew. A magnificent photograph records the day the heroes of the *Hopelyn* rescue received their medals. Striding proudly out of the gates of Buckingham Palace in 1924, after being presented with the honours by George V and accompanied by lifeboat men from Tynemouth and Fishguard, was a trio of courageous east coast coxswains. Watched by a police officer as they proudly left the palace in their uniforms and caps were Jack Swan and Billy Fleming; between them was Henry Blogg who had been presented with his Empire Gallantry Medal on that day. The ceremony was part of the celebrations marking the centenary of the lifeboat service.

*The lifeboats* Agnes Cross *(below) and* Kentwell *(above), both participants in the* Hopelyn *rescue.*

Fleming's 49-year career with the RNLI was one of valiant service that would place him second only to Henry Blogg in the list of Norfolk's most decorated lifeboat men.

Those who remember him recall him as a man

*Coxswains (from the left) Swan, Blogg and Fleming, together with fellow RNLI medal winners, leave Buckingham Palace after the centenary celebrations in 1924.*

who was full of fun yet lived his life for the lifeboat. His nephew Percy Burrage, who had grown up in the Fleming family home, once remarked: 'He was as pleased as Punch if he had saved anybody from a ship.'

Within the space of a gallant five years, Fleming achieved the full set of RNLI gallantry awards of Gold, Silver and Bronze medals. In 1926, when the Gorleston No 2 station was closed with the Gorleston No. 1 station renamed Great Yarmouth and Gorleston, he was awarded the Bronze Medal for the rescue of four crew from the ketch *Henrietta*. In 1927, he received the Silver Medal for his role in the rescue of the Dutch oil tanker *Georgia*.

Fleming retired from the service in 1934 and died in 1954 at the age of 89. Like many of the men who manned the lifeboats during that era, Fleming was a modest man. As with Blogg, he rarely wore his medals, only pinning them to his chest when he went to the Palace to collect another honour. The rest of the time, Coxswain Billy Fleming would keep them in a drawer at home, wrapped discreetly in a red and white handkerchief.

# CHAPTER TWENTY-FIVE

# *A. H. Taylor*

## (1886–1972)

Alfred Hugh Taylor had a military career that saw him present at some of the defining moments of the 20th century. Yet he also left a priceless legacy that helped maritime historians unlock the intricacies of the most significant naval battle of the 19th century.

As a naval officer he was despatched to Versailles in 1918 as part of the Royal Navy contingent that was drawing up the finer points of the Treaty of Versailles that would bring World War 1 to a close. Two decades later he was on the beaches of Dunkirk – a retired admiral brought back into service – co-ordinating the evacuation of British troops aboard the armada of little ships.

Admiral Taylor had a long and distinguished maritime career with the Royal Navy. He began his training back in the days when the Royal Navy still employed some vessels that relied entirely on wind-power. It may have seemed outdated, but what it did was ensure that Taylor and his contemporaries learned all the intricacies and nuances of handling a ship, before they later went on to command some of the finest warships of their day.

Alfred Hugh Taylor was born at Starston in the deep south of Norfolk close to the Suffolk border in 1886. He went to prep school in Eastbourne before going to HMS *Britannia*, the naval cadet training ship on the River Dart just below where Dartmouth College would eventually stand, in 1901. He went to sea in 1902–03 as a midshipman.

From the early days of his career, Taylor's expertise lay in torpedoes and he spent much of World War 1 as a staff officer at HMS *Vernon* – the navy's torpedo

*Admiral Taylor's service combined action at sea, diplomacy at the Versailles Peace Conference and research to apply his knowledge of maritime history, particularly to Wyllie's great Trafalgar panorama.*

school in Portsmouth – checking the torpedo systems on new vessels before they were handed over to their captains.

He later became involved in the peace process and for his services at the Versailles Peace Conference during the final stages of the war he was awarded an OBE in 1919.

After World War 1 he had a spell on the staff of the commander-in-chief of the Atlantic Fleet before becoming a commander on HMS *Royal Oak* in the 1920s. That was one of the happiest periods of his career and he had a strong affinity with that vessel. The battleship was sunk after being torpedoed by a German U-boat while at anchor at Scapa Flow off the Orkneys on 14th October 1939, with 833 casualties. Taylor's son John – who served in the Royal Navy from 1944 to 1953 as a Lieutenant – recalls his father being 'utterly shattered' when he heard the news that the *Royal Oak* had gone down with such a catastrophic loss of life.

Taylor captained HMS *Delhi* in 1927–28 and later served as captain of HMS *Stuart* – a destroyer flotilla leader, with eight ships in the flotilla. He was also captain of *Vernon* and then of the HMS *Valiant* in 1935.

Alongside a highly successful and active naval career, Admiral Taylor was also an enthusiastic naval historian and it was this love of the exploits of his forebears, coupled with a friendship with the renowned maritime artist W. L. Wyllie, that was to unlock the uncertainties of perhaps the greatest sea battle of all time – Trafalgar.

When Admiral Taylor learned that Wyllie had been commissioned to paint the Battle of Trafalgar, he was only too happy to offer his services and apply his knowledge of maritime history to the task as a researcher. The two families were closely linked. Wyllie's son Harold was godfather to Taylor's son John. John Taylor was also taught at primary school by Wyllie's daughter Aileen.

Taylor's aim was simple – his prime concern was to enable Wyllie to depict a highly accurate painted version of Nelson's victory over the combined French and Spanish fleets. The fact that what emerged from the research was to become the definitive version of the Battle of Trafalgar was little more than a convenient by-product of what had been a joyous and enthralling task as far as Admiral Taylor was concerned.

The work began in earnest while A. H. Taylor was a commander at the Admiralty, and reached full steam as he made his way to China as captain on HMS *Delhi* in 1927. Much of it was appropriately conducted at sea when his day's work as captain was completed and he had time to read. Taylor went to great lengths to ensure that the account – and subsequently the painting – was extremely accurate.

He read through the log books of all the ships at Trafalgar – the 33 French and Spanish ships and the 27 from Nelson's fleet – to work out where they were at any particular moment in the battle. That research extended to Taylor learning enough of the languages of the enemy captains to enable him to follow the log books of their ships for himself. From there, he worked out a meticulous plan of the battle that was then used to establish the view that went into Wyllie's painting.

Yet there were other obstacles in his drive for accuracy. It emerged that the time keeping on some of the ships was rudimentary, making it doubly difficult to match times and positions. There were cases of ships that recorded that they were shooting at one another but had listed different times for the engagement. The light winds at Trafalgar and the slow drifting smoke from the cannons added a further dimension to the problem. Taylor suspected that some ships had found difficulty in visually identifying exactly which vessel they were firing at. This prompted some highly detailed maritime detective work by Taylor to try to clarify precisely which ship was engaged by which other.

Once Taylor was satisfied with his work in piecing together the unfolding events, he offered a plan from which Wyllie was able to paint his picture of the Battle of Trafalgar. Wyllie duly rewarded Taylor, permitting him to paint three of the frigates on the skyline in the panorama!

Wyllie, who was later an important figure in the eventual restoration of Nelson's flagship HMS *Victory*, completed his painting in 1930. It is one of the most celebrated paintings of the Battle of Trafalgar, an acknowledged masterpiece of maritime art. At 42 feet (13m) long, it can now be seen in the Royal Naval Museum in Portsmouth.

On retirement, A. H. Taylor was promoted to the rank of rear admiral as the navy's most senior serving captain at the time and returned to the family home in Diss, where he put together his paper on the Battle of Trafalgar for the Society for Nautical Research. The work was ready for publication, even the plates were made up for the printing process, when World War 2 intervened resulting in the project being put on hold. His work, although preserved in Wyllie's painting, later became a casualty of war when the print works was bombed and his account of Trafalgar went up in smoke.

As early as 1938, with the threat of war again looming across Europe, A. H. Taylor had been recalled to the service as a commodore in the Royal Naval Reserve. He held a number of positions throughout the war. An early role was in the evacuation from the beaches in Dunkirk in 1940. Taylor was a key player in organising the despatch of the little ships to rescue thousands of British troops who had been pushed back to the coastline by the advancing German army.

Based at Sheerness in Kent, he eventually went over to Dunkirk himself to co-ordinate the operation from the beaches and was mentioned in dispatches for his part in the evacuation.

He later had a job in the Ministry of Economic Warfare plotting the movement of the German merchant ships and was also Chief of Staff to the Commander-in-Chief in Chatham who oversaw the eastern coastline of Britain and all the wartime convoys that passed through it. Later, he went to be naval director of the SOE (Special Operations Executive), planning sabotage missions across Europe. It was a role that he regarded as so secret and sensitive that he never spoke of it, even to his family.

After the war, Taylor returned to matters Trafalgar and rewrote his paper for the Society for Nautical Research. This led to the publication of what has become a definitive version of the Battle of Trafalgar in the *Mariner's Mirror* in 1950.

*Artist W. L. Wyllie at work by the waterside.*

The work has been referred to since by authorities on Trafalgar and by several leading authors who produced books on Nelson, his battles and life, notably those published to coincide with the 200th anniversary of the Battle of Trafalgar in 2005.

Admiral Taylor is commemorated in the Corn Hall, Diss, where his painting still hangs. He spent much of his retirement in local politics, serving as a Norfolk County Councillor for Diss for 30 years from 1938 and sitting on committees for education, planning, and finance and general purposes. He was elected Alderman and also served on the urban district council. He was a J.P. from 1937 to 1961, a deputy lord lieutenant from 1951 to 1961 and died in 1972, aged 85.

*Wyllie and his wife in old age.*

# CHAPTER TWENTY-SIX

# *Steve Burgoine*

## (1948– )

In attaining the rank of Commodore of the P&O fleet, Steve Burgoine followed in the tradition of some of Britain's more illustrious mariners from the great ocean-going liner fleets.

For many years as P&O's senior captain, he commanded the operator's newest vessels as they were launched onto the world market – vessels bearing legendary names such as *Oriana*, *Aurora*, *Oceana* and currently *Arcadia*. He steered them through high profile launches, and equally high profile 'teething problems' in a manner that maintained the integrity of his status and of the operator. His appointment as Commodore in January 2007 was the pinnacle of a career that began in the lower ranks of merchant shipping fleets and it is that which sets him apart.

Born at Earlham Hall in Norwich, he is the son of a prominent architect in the city. His grandfather was a master tailor and ran a gentleman's outfitters called Greens in Gentleman's Walk. Educated at Bracondale School in Norwich, he undertook his merchant navy academic studies at HMS *Worcester* at the Thames Nautical Training College before joining P&O Cruises in 1966 as a deck cadet sailing on *Soudan*, *Ballarat* and *Chusan*. In announcing the 2007 promotion, Lloyd's List noted that Commodore Burgoine was the only seagoing Old Worcester in the P&O fleet (HMS *Worcester* had closed in 1968).

In 1969, he was promoted to Fourth, and then Third Officer and served on *Orcadea*, *Strathconon* and various other cargo vessels from the P&O Cargo Division fleet. In 1972, Burgoine took time out from sea travel and embarked on a degree course in Maritime Studies at the University of Wales. Three years later he returned to P&O Cruises as Second Officer and served on board the original *Oriana* and *Canberra*. He was then promoted to First Officer on board both ships.

From 1977 onwards, Burgoine served in positions ranking from First Officer up to Chief Officer on various vessels, including *Island Princess*, the original *Sun Princess*, *Pacific Princess*, the original *Oriana*, *Canberra*, *Royal Princess* and *Sky Princess*. In 1991 he was promoted to deputy captain, serving on board *Canberra*, *Sky Princess* and *Royal Princess* (now *Artemis*).

After a spell serving as the owner's representative in the original *Golden Princess*, he was promoted to the position of captain, and to his first command, on board *Pacific Princess* in 1996. He has since served as captain on board *Victoria*, *Island Princess*, *Oriana*, *Aurora*, *Oceana* and *Arcadia*, his current ship, of which he took the helm in April 2005.

Commodore Burgoine is a Member of the Royal Institution of Naval Architects and a Fellow of the Royal Institute of Navigation. He has also been made a Freeman of the City of London.

The promotion to Commodore was in recognition of Burgoine's exemplary service over four decades. He has taken the helm of P&O's latest launches and navigated them through the very public problems that can face a new ship on a maiden voyage. As captain of the £200m superliner *Aurora* in 2000, which broke down on its maiden voyage, Burgoine guided the 76,000-tonne vessel into a German port for repairs. That enabled her to get back into Southampton in time to depart on a second scheduled sailing to the Canary Islands, with more than 1,800 passengers on board, helping head off a potential public relations disaster for P&O. At the time, he said of the breakdown: 'Embarrassing is the wrong word, but it is very disappointing.'

In becoming commodore, he attains a rank that is steeped in history with its roots in the French orders of chivalry. It was first used in Britain by King William III, a rank adopted not only by the Royal Navy but also by merchant shipping companies.

On the great passenger liners in the heyday of the 1920s and 1930s, the commodores – especially those commanding liners on the passage between Southampton and New York – were held in high social regard. Several of the men who occupied such positions were larger than life characters, often making the headlines in their own right.

In fact, the position of Commodore of Cunard was once so prestigious that those elevated to such rank were customarily knighted. They included Sir Arthur

*Steve Burgoine, Commodore of the P&O fleet.*

Rostron, who had been master of the *Carpathia* when in 1912 she sped through the Arctic night to rescue the survivors of the *Titanic*. Commodore Sir James Bissett commanded the former *Queen Mary* from 1944 to 1947 and during the latter stages of World War 2, carrying GIs from America to Europe and outrunning enemy U-boats at a speed of more than 30 knots.

Most other cruise lines now do not have commodores, the exceptions being P&O and Cunard, which appointed the Master of the *Queen Mary 2* Bernard Warner as its new commodore at the same time as Commodore Burgoine's elevation. The position of Commodore for Burgoine saw the man who began his maritime career as a deck cadet, become the Senior Master of the P&O Cruises fleet. It is a rank awarded to a captain with an exemplary service record and the position is the highest rank attainable within the P&O fleet. When the news of the promotion came through, Burgoine was where he is most comfortable, at the helm of a P&O liner – at that time he happened to be halfway between Aruba and Trinidad in the Caribbean on the *Arcadia*. The 83,000-tonne vessel he commands has 11 decks, 880 crew, is 285 metres long with a cruising speed of 22 knots and its 976 cabins have a regular passenger capacity of 1,952. While continuing as captain of the *Arcadia*, Commodore Burgoine's extended role is to represent the interests of all ships and their captains.

*Commodore Burgoine on the bridge of the* Arcadia.

P&O Cruises, which has been operating cruise ships for more than 170 years, has a fleet of six ships dedicated to the British market and serving destinations including the Caribbean, South America, Scandinavia, Mediterranean, Atlantic Islands and round-the-world cruises. The latest, the 290-

# *Bibliography and Sources*

**Archives**

The Burney Centre, McGill University, Montreal, Canada

Churchill Archive Centre, Cambridge (papers of 1st Sea Lord Fisher of Kilverstone)

Thomas Crisp jnr, memoirs and private papers (1958) (private repository with his granddaughter Doreen Hague)

Norfolk Heritage Centre

Norfolk Museums Service

Norfolk Record Office

**Books**

G. H. Anderson, *Vancouver and his Great Voyage: the Story of a Norfolk Sailor* (King's Lynn: Thew & Son, 1923)

Martin Brayne, *The Greatest Storm: Britain's Night of Destruction, November 1703* (Stroud: Sutton Publishing, 2002)

George Christopher Davies, *The Handbook to the Rivers and Broads of Norfolk & Suffolk* (London: Jarrold & Sons, 1882)

Frank L. Fox, *A Distant Storm: the Four Days' Battle of 1666* (Rotherfield: Press of Sail Publications, 1996)

Simon Harris, *Sir Cloudesley Shovell – Stuart Admiral* (Staplehurst: Spellmount, 2000)

Dominick Harrod (ed.), *War, Ice and Piracy: the Remarkable Career of a Victorian Sailor: the Journals and Letters of Samuel Gurney Cresswell* (London: Chatham Publishing, 2000)

Henry Hibberd, *A History of Burnham Thorpe* (Norwich: Goose, 1937)

Cyril Jolly, *Henry Blogg of Cromer: the Greatest of the Lifeboat-men* (Cromer: Poppyland Publishing, 2002)

R. W. Ketton-Cremer, *Felbrigg: the Story of a House* (London: Hart-Davis, 1962)

Andrew Lambert, *Nelson: Britannia's God of War* (London: Faber and Faber, 2004)

J. M. Lambert, *The Making of the Broads* (Royal Geographical Society, 1962).

Charles Lewis, *Nelson: 'I am myself a Norfolk man'* (Cromer: Poppyland Publishing, 2005)

Charles Lewis, *Nelson's Monument, Great Yarmouth* (Norfolk Museums Service, 1985)

Ebenezer Mather, *'Nor'ard of the Dogger'* (James Nisbet, 1887)

Tom Pocock, *Nelson and his World* (London: Thames and Hudson, 1968)

Tom Pocock, *Horatio Nelson* (London: Pimlico, 1994)

N. A. M. Rodger, *The Command of the Ocean: a Naval History of Britain, 1649–1815* (London: Penguin, 2005)

Ernest Suffling, *The Land of the Broads – A Practical and Illustrated Guide* (Startford: Benjamin Perry, 1892)

Howard Swales, 'Captain Manby', *Norfolk Fair* August 1971.

George Vancouver, *A Voyage of Discovery to the North Pacific Ocean and Round the World 1791–1795* (ed. W. Kaye Lamb) (London: Hakluyt Society, 1984)

Oliver Warner, *A Portrait of Lord Nelson* (London: Chatto and Windus, 1958)

Colin White (ed.), *Nelson: The New Letters* (Woodbridge: Boydell Press, 2005)

Colin White and the 1805 Club, *The Trafalgar Captains: their Lives and Memorials* (London: Chatham Publishing, 2005)

## Periodicals
*Eastern Daily Press*
*London Gazette*
*Mariner's Mirror*
*Norfolk Life*
*The Times*

## Websites
Cutty Sark: www.cuttysark.org.uk

National Maritime Museum: www.nmm.ac.uk

National Trust: www.nationaltrust.org.uk

P&O Cruises: www.pocruises.com

*The Diary of Samuel Pepys*, www.pepysdiary.com

Poppyland Publishing: www.poppyland.co.uk

Red Duster (The Merchant Navy Association): www.red-duster.co.uk

RNLI: www.rnli.org.uk

Royal National Mission to Deep Sea Fishermen: www.fishermensmission.org.uk

# Index

To help family and local historians, names of Norfolk people are indexed even when the text refers to them only in passing; likewise, those interested in maritime history will find in the index all names of ships, set in italics; and the inclusion of so many placenames shows the worldwide nature of Norfolk's maritime connections.

169